Ponkapog Edition

THE WRITINGS OF

THOMAS BAILEY ALDRICH

IN NINE VOLUMES

WITH PORTRAITS AND MANY ILLUSTRATIONS

VOLUME IX

THE WRITINGS
OF
THOMAS BAILEY ALDRICH

PONKAPOG PAPERS, A SEA TURN, AND OTHER PAPERS

BOSTON AND NEW YORK
HOUGHTON, MIFFLIN AND COMPANY
THE RIVERSIDE PRESS, CAMBRIDGE
1907

CONTENTS

	PAGE
PONKAPOG PAPERS	
LEAVES FROM A NOTE BOOK	1
ASIDES	43
TOM FOLIO	45
FLEABODY AND OTHER QUEER NAMES	54
A NOTE ON "L'AIGLON"	57
PLOT AND CHARACTER	62
THE CRUELTY OF SCIENCE	64
LEIGH HUNT AND BARRY CORNWALL	69
DECORATION DAY	74
WRITERS AND TALKERS	77
ON EARLY RISING	79
UN POÊTE MANQUÉ	83
THE MALE COSTUME OF THE PERIOD	87
ON A CERTAIN AFFECTATION	91
WISHMAKERS' TOWN	95
HISTORICAL NOVELS	100
POOR YORICK	103
THE AUTOGRAPH HUNTER	108
ROBERT HERRICK	115
A SEA TURN AND OTHER MATTERS	
A SEA TURN	151
HIS GRACE THE DUKE	194

SHAW'S FOLLY 211
AN UNTOLD STORY 263
THE CASE OF THOMAS PHIPPS 273
THE WHITE FEATHER 298
INDEX TO TITLES OF THE PROSE WORKS . 317

ILLUSTRATIONS

REDMAN FARM, MR. ALDRICH'S HOME AT PONKAPOG . . . . *Frontispiece*
From a photograph by I. Chester Horton.

LEIGH HUNT 70
From the original painting by Samuel Lawrence.
The last stanza of "Abou Ben-Adhem" is from an autograph copy of the poem in the possession of Mrs. T. B. Aldrich.

BOOTH'S ROOM IN "THE PLAYERS" CLUB, NEW YORK CITY 104
From a photograph by N. L. Stebbins. On a bracket at the right of the fireplace is shown the skull Mr. Booth used in the grave-digging scene in "Hamlet."

THE BETHULÎA, MR. TALBOT ALDRICH'S YACHT 152
Of the two figures which stand out on the yacht, the one nearer the stern is Mr. T. B. Aldrich.

PONKAPOG PAPERS

To

FRANCIS BARTLETT

THESE miscellaneous notes and essays are called "Ponkapog Papers," not simply because they chanced, for the most part, to be written within the limits of the old Indian Reservation, but, rather, because there is something typical of their unpretentiousness in the modesty with which Ponkapog assumes to being even a village. The little Massachusetts settlement, nestled under the wing of the Blue Hills, has no illusions concerning itself, never mistakes the cackle of the bourg for the sound that echoes round the world, and no more thinks of rivaling great centres of human activity than these slight papers dream of inviting comparison between themselves and important pieces of literature. Therefore there seems something especially appropriate in the geographical title selected; and if the author's choice of name need further excuse, it is to be found in the alluring alliteration lying ready at his hand.

REDMAN FARM, *Ponkapog*,
1903

LEAVES FROM A NOTE BOOK

LEAVES FROM A NOTE BOOK

In his Memoirs, Kropótkin states the singular fact that the natives of the Malayan Archipelago have an idea that something is extracted from them when their likenesses are taken by photography. Here is the motive for a fantastic short story, in which the hero — an author in vogue or a popular actor — might be depicted as having all his good qualities gradually photographed out of him. This could well be the result of too prolonged indulgence in the effort to "look natural." First the man loses his charming simplicity; then he begins to pose in intellectual attitudes, with finger on brow; then he becomes morbidly self-conscious, and finally ends in an asylum for incurable egotists. His death might be brought about by a cold caught in going out bareheaded, there being, for the moment, no hat in the market of sufficient circumference to meet his enlarged requirement.

The evening we dropped anchor in the Bay of Yedo the moon was hanging directly over

Yokohama. It was a mother-of-pearl moon, and might have been manufactured by any of the delicate artisans in the Hanchodori quarter. It impressed one as being a very good imitation, but nothing more. Nammikawa, the cloisonné-worker at Tokio, could have made a better moon.

I NOTICE the announcement of a new edition of "The Two First Centuries of Florentine Literature," by Professor Pasquale Villari. I am not acquainted with the work in question, but I trust that Professor Villari makes it plain to the reader how both centuries happened to be first.

THE walking delegates of a higher civilization, who have nothing to divide, look upon the notion of property as a purely artificial creation of human society. According to these advanced philosophers, the time will come when no man shall be allowed to call anything his. The beneficent law which takes away an author's rights in his own books just at the period when old age is creeping upon him, seems to me a handsome stride toward the longed-for millennium.

SAVE us from our friends — our enemies we can guard against. The well-meaning rector of the little parish of Woodgates, England, and several of Robert Browning's local admirers, have recently busied themselves in erecting a tablet to the memory of "the first known forefather of the poet." This lately turned up ancestor, who does not date very far back, was also named Robert Browning, and is described on the mural marble as "formerly footman and butler to Sir John Bankes of Corfe Castle." Now, Robert Browning, the poet, had as good right as Abou Ben Adhem himself to ask to be placed on the list of those who love their fellow men; but if the poet could have been consulted in the matter, he probably would have preferred not to have that particular footman exhumed. However, it is an ill wind that blows nobody good. Sir John Bankes would scarcely have been heard of in our young century if it had not been for his footman. As Robert stood day by day, sleek and solemn, behind his master's chair in Corfe Castle, how little it entered into the head of Sir John that his highly respectable name would be served up to posterity — like a cold relish — by his own butler! By Robert!

In the East-Side slums of New York, somewhere in the picturesque Bowery district, stretches a malodorous little street wholly given over to long-bearded, bird-beaked merchants of ready-made and second-hand clothing. The contents of the dingy shops seem to have revolted, and rushed pell-mell out of doors, and taken possession of the sidewalk. One could fancy that the rebellion had been quelled at this point, and that those ghastly rows of complete suits strung up on either side of the doorways were the bodies of the seditious ringleaders. But as you approach these limp figures, each dangling and gyrating on its cord in a most suggestive fashion, you notice, pinned to the lapel of a coat here and there, a strip of paper announcing the very low price at which you may become the happy possessor. That dissipates the illusion.

Polonius, in the play, gets killed — and not any too soon. If it only were practicable to kill him in real life! A story — to be called "The Passing of Polonius" — in which a king issues a decree condemning to death every long-winded, didactic person in the kingdom, irrespective of rank, and is himself instantly arrested and decapitated. The man who suspects his own tediousness is yet to be born.

Whenever I take up Emerson's poems I find myself turning automatically to his "Bacchus."

Elsewhere, in detachable passages embedded in mediocre verse, he rises for a moment to heights not reached by any other of our poets; but "Bacchus" is in the grand style throughout. Its texture can bear comparison with the world's best in this kind. In imaginative quality and austere richness of diction, what other verse of our period approaches it? The day Emerson wrote "Bacchus" he had in him, as Michael Drayton said of Marlowe, "those brave translunary things that the first poets had."

Imagine all human beings swept off the face of the earth excepting one man. Imagine this man in some vast city, New York or London. Imagine him on the third or fourth day of his solitude sitting in a house and hearing a ring at the door-bell!

No man has ever yet succeeded in painting an honest portrait of himself in an autobiography, however sedulously he may have set to work about it. In spite of his candid purpose he omits necessary touches and adds superfluous ones. At times he cannot help draping his thought, and the least shred of drapery becomes a disguise. It is only the diarist who accomplishes the feat of self-portraiture, and he, without any such end in view, does it unconsciously.

A man cannot keep a daily record of his comings and goings and the little items that make up the sum of his life, and not inadvertently betray himself at every turn. He lays bare his heart with a candor not possible to the self-consciousness that inevitably colors premeditated revelation. While Pepys was filling those small octavo pages with his perplexing cipher he never once suspected that he was adding a photographic portrait of himself to the world's gallery of immortals. We are more intimately acquainted with Mr. Samuel Pepys, the inner man — his little meannesses and his large generosities — than we are with half the persons we call our dear friends.

THE young girl in my story is to be as sensitive to praise as a prism is to light. Whenever anybody praises her she breaks into colors.

IN the process of dusting my study, the other morning, the maid replaced an engraving of Philip II of Spain upside down on the mantel-shelf, and His Majesty has remained in that undignified posture ever since. I have no disposition to come to his aid. My abhorrence of the wretch is as hearty as if he had not been dead and — otherwise provided for these last three hundred years. Bloody Mary of England was nearly as merciless, but she was sincere and uncompromising in her extirpation of heretics. Philip II, whose one recorded hearty laugh was occasioned by the news of the St. Bartholomew massacre, could mask his fanaticism or drop it for the time being, when it seemed politic to do so. Queen Mary was a maniac; but the successor of Torquemada was the incarnation of cruelty pure and simple, and I have a mind to let my counterfeit presentment of him stand on its head for the rest of its natural life. I cordially dislike several persons, but I hate nobody, living or dead, excepting Philip II of Spain. He appears to give me as much trouble as Charles I gave the amiable Mr. Dick.

Among the delightful men and women whom you are certain to meet at an English country-house there is generally one guest who is supposed to be preternaturally clever and amusing — "so very droll, don't you know?" He recites things, tells stories in costermonger dialect, and mimics public characters. He is a type of a class, and I take him to be one of the elementary forms of animal life, like the acalephæ. His presence is capable of adding a gloom to an undertaker's establishment. The last time I fell in with him was on a coaching trip through Devon, and in spite of what I have said I must confess to receiving an instant of entertainment at his hands. He was delivering a little dissertation on "the English and American languages." As there were two Americans on the back seat — it seems we term ourselves "Amurricans" — his choice of subject was full of tact. It was exhilarating to get a lesson in pronunciation from a gentleman who said *boult* for bolt, called St. John *Sin' Jun*, and did not know how to pronounce the beautiful name of his own college at Oxford. Fancy a perfectly sober man saying *Maudlin* for Magdalen! Perhaps the purest English spoken is that of the English folk who have resided abroad ever since the Elizabethan period, or thereabouts.

Every one has a bookplate these days, and the collectors are after it. The fool and his bookplate are soon parted. To distribute one's *ex-libris* is inanely to destroy the only significance it has, that of indicating the past or present ownership of the volume in which it is placed.

When an Englishman is not highly imaginative he is apt to be the most matter-of-fact of mortals. He is rarely imaginative, and seldom has an alert sense of humor. Yet England has produced the finest of humorists and the greatest of poets. The humor and imagination which are diffused through other peoples concentrate themselves from time to time in individual Englishmen.

This is a page of autobiography, though not written in the first person: Many years ago a noted Boston publisher used to keep a large memorandum-book on a table in his personal office. The volume always lay open, and was in no manner a private affair, being the receptacle of nothing more important than hastily-scrawled reminders to attend to this thing or the other. It chanced one day that a very young, unfledged author, passing through the city, looked in upon the publisher, who was also the editor of a famous magazine. The unfledged had a copy of verses secreted about his person. The publisher was absent, and young Milton, feeling that "they also serve who only stand and wait," sat down and waited. Presently his eye fell upon the memorandum-book, lying there spread out like a morning newspaper, and almost in spite of himself he read: "Don't forget to see the binder," "Don't forget to mail E—— his contract," "Don't forget H——'s proofs," etc. An inspiration seized upon the youth; he took a pencil, and at the tail of this long list of "don't forgets" he wrote: "Don't forget to accept

A——'s poem." He left his manuscript on the table and disappeared. That afternoon, when the publisher glanced over his memoranda, he was not a little astonished at the last item; but his sense of humor was so strong that he did accept the poem (it required a strong sense of humor to do that), and sent the lad a check for it, though the verses remain to this day unprinted. That kindly publisher was wise as well as kind.

FRENCH novels with metaphysical or psychological prefaces are always certain to be particularly indecent.

I HAVE lately discovered that Master Harry Sandford of England, the priggish little boy in the story of "Sandford and Merton," has a worthy American cousin in one Elsie Dinsmore, who sedately pirouettes through a seemingly endless succession of girls' books. I came across a nest of fifteen of them the other day. This impossible female is carried from infancy up to grandmotherhood, and is, I believe, still leisurely pursuing her way down to the tomb in an ecstatic state of uninterrupted didacticism. There are twenty-five volumes of her and the granddaughter, who is also christened Elsie, and is her grandmother's own child, with the same precocious readiness to dispense ethical instruction to her elders. An interesting instance of hereditary talent!

H——'s intellect resembles a bamboo—slender, graceful, and hollow. Personally, he is long and narrow, and looks as if he might have been the product of a rope-walk. He is loosely put together, like an ill-constructed sentence, and affects me like one. His figure is ungrammatical.

AMERICAN humor is nearly as ephemeral as the flowers that bloom in the spring. Each generation has its own crop, and, as a rule, insists on cultivating a new kind. That of 1860, if it were to break into blossom at the present moment, would probably be left to fade upon the stem. Humor is a delicate shrub, with the passing hectic flush of its time. The current-topic variety is especially subject to very early frosts, as is also the dialectic species. Mark Twain's humor is not to be classed with the fragile plants; it has a serious root striking deep down into rich earth, and I think it will go on flowering indefinitely.

I HAVE been imagining an ideal critical journal, whose plan should involve the discharge of the chief literary critic and the installment of a fresh censor on the completion of each issue. To place a man in permanent absolute control of a certain number of pages, in which to express his opinions, is to place him in a position of great personal danger. It is almost inevitable that he should come to overrate the importance of those opinions, to take himself with far too much seriousness, and in the end adopt the dogma of his own infallibility. The liberty to summon this or that man-of-letters to a supposititious bar of justice is apt to beget in the self-appointed judge an exaggerated sense of superiority. He becomes impatient of any rulings not his, and says in effect, if not in so many words: "I am Sir Oracle, and when I ope my lips let no dog bark." When the critic reaches this exalted frame of mind his slight usefulness is gone.

AFTER a debauch of thunder-shower, the weather takes the pledge and signs it with a rainbow.

I LIKE to have a thing suggested rather than told in full. When every detail is given, the mind rests satisfied, and the imagination loses the desire to use its own wings. The partly draped statue has a charm which the nude lacks. Who would have those marble folds slip from the raised knee of the Venus of Melos? Hawthorne knew how to make his lovely thought lovelier by sometimes half veiling it.

I HAVE just tested the nib of a new pen on a slight fancy which Herrick has handled twice in the "Hesperides." The fancy, however, is not Herrick's; it is as old as poetry and the exaggeration of lovers, and I have the same privilege as another to try my fortune with it:

UP ROOS THE SONNE, AND UP ROOS EMELYE

CHAUCER

When some hand has partly drawn
  The cloudy curtains of her bed,
  And my lady's golden head
Glimmers in the dusk like dawn,
Then methinks is day begun.
Later, when her dream has ceased
  And she softly stirs and wakes,
Then it is as when the East
  A sudden rosy magic takes
From the cloud-enfolded sun,
  And full day breaks!

Shakespeare, who has done so much to discourage literature by anticipating everybody, puts the whole matter into a nutshell:

But soft! what light through yonder window breaks?
It is the east, and Juliet is the sun.

There is a phrase spoken by Hamlet which I have seen quoted innumerable times, and never once correctly. Hamlet, addressing Horatio, says:

> Give me that man
> That is not passion's slave, and I will wear him
> In my heart's core, ay, in my *heart of heart.*

The words italicized are invariably written "heart of hearts"—as if a person possessed that organ in duplicate. Perhaps no one living, with the exception of Sir Henry Irving, is more familiar with the play of "Hamlet" than my good friend Mr. Bram Stoker, who makes his heart plural on two occasions in his recent novel, "The Mystery of the Sea." Mrs. Humphry Ward also twice misquotes the passage in "Lady Rose's Daughter."

Books that have become classics—books that have had their day and now get more praise than perusal—always remind me of venerable colonels and majors and captains who, having reached the age limit, find themselves retired upon half pay.

Whether or not the fretful porcupine rolls itself into a ball is a subject over which my friend John Burroughs and several brother naturalists have lately become as heated as if the question involved points of theology. Up among the Adirondacks, and in the very heart of the region of porcupines, I happen to have a modest cottage. This retreat is called "The Porcupine," and I ought by good rights to know something about the habits of the small animal from which it derives its name. Last winter my dog Buster used to return home on an average of three times a month from an excursion up Mt. Pisgah with his nose stuck full of quills, and *he* ought to have some concrete ideas on the subject. We two, then, are prepared to testify that the porcupine in its moments of relaxation occasionally contracts itself into what might be taken for a ball by persons not too difficult to please in the matter of spheres. But neither Buster nor I — being unwilling to get into trouble — would like to assert that it is an actual ball. That it is a shape with which one had better not thoughtlessly meddle is a conviction that my friend Buster stands ready to defend against all comers.

WORDSWORTH'S characterization of the woman in one of his poems as "a creature not too bright or good for human nature's daily food" has always appeared to me too cannibalesque to be poetical. It directly sets one to thinking of the South Sea Islanders.

Though Iago was not exactly the kind of person one would select as a superintendent for a Sunday School, his advice to young Roderigo was wisdom itself — "Put money in thy purse." Whoever disparages money disparages every step in the progress of the human race. I listened the other day to a sermon in which gold was personified as a sort of glittering devil tempting mortals to their ruin. I had an instant of natural hesitation when the contribution plate was passed around immediately afterward. Personally, I believe that the possession of gold has ruined fewer men than the lack of it. What noble enterprises have been checked and what fine souls have been blighted in the gloom of poverty, the world will never know. "After the love of knowledge," says Buckle, "there is no one passion which has done so much good to mankind as the love of money."

Dialect tempered with slang is an admirable medium of communication between persons who have nothing to say and persons who would not care for anything properly said.

Dr. Holmes had an odd liking for ingenious desk-accessories in the way of pencil-sharpeners, paper-weights, penholders, etc. The latest contrivances in this fashion — probably dropped down to him by the inventor angling for a nibble of commendation — were always making one another's acquaintance on his study table. He once said to me: "I 'm waiting for somebody to invent a mucilage-brush that you can't by any accident put into your inkstand. It would save me frequent moments of humiliation."

The deceptive Mr. False and the volatile Mrs. Giddy, who figure in the pages of seventeenth and eighteenth century fiction, are not tolerated in modern novels and plays. Steal, the burglar, and Palette, the artist, have ceased to be. A name indicating the quality or occupation of the bearer strikes us as a too transparent device. Yet there are such names in contemporary real life. That of our worthy Adjutant-General Drum may be instanced. Neal and Pray are a pair of deacons who linger in the memory of my boyhood. Sweet, the confectioner, and Lamb, the butcher, are individuals with whom I have had dealings. The old-time sign of Ketchum and Cheetam, Brokers, in Wall Street, New York, seems almost too good to be true. But it was once, if it is not now, an actuality.

I HAVE observed that whenever a Boston author dies, New York immediately becomes a great literary centre.

THE possession of unlimited power will make a despot of almost any man. There is a possible Nero in the gentlest human creature that walks.

EVERY living author has a projection of himself, a sort of eidolon, that goes about in near and remote places making friends or enemies for him among persons who never lay eyes upon the writer in the flesh. When he dies, this phantasmal personality fades away, and the author lives only in the impression created by his own literature. It is only then that the world begins to perceive what manner of man the poet, the novelist, or the historian really was. Not until he is dead, and perhaps some long time dead, is it possible for the public to take his exact measure. Up to that point contemporary criticism has either overrated him or underrated him, or ignored him altogether, having been misled by the eidolon, which always plays fantastic tricks with the writer temporarily under its dominion. It invariably represents him as either a greater or a smaller personage than he actually is. Presently the simulacrum works no more spells, good or evil, and the deception is unveiled. The hitherto disregarded author is recognized, and the idol of yesterday, which seemed so important, is taken down from his too large pedestal and carted off to the dumping-ground of inadequate things. To be sure, if he chances to have been not entirely unworthy, and on cool examination is found to possess some appreciable degree of merit, then he is set up on a new slab of appropriate dimensions. The late colossal statue shrinks to a modest bas-relief. On the other hand, some scarcely noticed bust may suddenly become a revered full-length figure. Between the reputation of the author living and the reputation of the same author dead there is ever a wide discrepancy.

A NOT too enchanting glimpse of Tennyson is incidentally given by Charles Brookfield, the English actor, in his "Random Recollections." Mr. Brookfield's father was, on one occasion, dining at the Oxford and Cambridge Club with George Venables, Frank Lushington, Alfred Tennyson, and others. "After dinner," relates the random recollector, "the poet insisted upon putting his feet on the table, tilting back his chair *more Americano*. There were strangers in the room, and he was expostulated with for his uncouthness, but in vain. 'Do put down your feet!' pleaded his host. 'Why should I?' retorted Tennyson. 'I'm very comfortable as I am.' 'Every one's staring at you,' said another. 'Let 'em stare,' replied the poet, placidly. 'Alfred,' said my father, 'people will think you're Longfellow.' Down went the feet." That *more Americano* of Brookfield the younger is delicious with its fine insular flavor, but the holding up of Longfellow — the soul of gentleness, the prince of courtesy — as a bugaboo of bad manners is simply inimitable. It will take England years and years to detect the full unconscious humor of it.

Great orators who are not also great writers become very indistinct historical shadows to the generations immediately following them. The spell vanishes with the voice. A man's voice is almost the only part of him entirely obliterated by death. The violet of his native land may be made of his ashes, but nature in her economy seems to have taken no care of his intonations, unless she perpetuates them in restless waves of air surging about the poles. The well-graced actor who leaves no perceptible record of his genius has a decided advantage over the mere orator. The tradition of the player's method and presence is associated with works of enduring beauty. Turning to the pages of the dramatist, we can picture to ourselves the greatness of Garrick or Siddons in this or that scene, in this or that character. It is not so easy to conjure up the impassioned orator from the pages of a dry and possibly illogical argument in favor of or against some long-ago-exploded measure of government. The laurels of an orator who is not a master of literary art wither quickly.

All the best sands of my life are somehow getting into the wrong end of the hour-glass. If I could only reverse it! Were it in my power to do so, would I?

Shakespeare is forever coming into our affairs — putting in his oar, so to speak — with some pat word or sentence. The conversation, the other evening, had turned on the subject of watches, when one of the gentlemen present, the manager of a large watch-making establishment, told us a rather interesting fact. The component parts of a watch are produced by different workmen, who have no concern with the complex piece of mechanism as a whole, and possibly, as a rule, understand it imperfectly. Each worker needs to be expert in only his own special branch. When the watch has reached a certain advanced state, the work requires a touch as delicate and firm as that of an oculist performing an operation. Here the most skilled and trustworthy artisans are employed; they receive high wages, and have the benefit of a singular indulgence. In case the workman, through too continuous application, finds himself lacking the steadiness of nerve demanded by his task, he is allowed without forfeiture of pay to remain idle temporarily, in order that his hand may recover the requisite precision of touch. As I listened, Hamlet's courtly criticism of the grave-digger's want of sensibility came drifting into my memory. "The hand of little employment hath the daintier sense," says Shakespeare, who has left nothing unsaid.

It was a festival in honor of Dai Butsu or some one of the auxiliary deities that preside over the destinies of Japland. For three days and nights the streets of Tokio — where the squat little brown houses look for all the world as if they were mimicking the favorite sitting posture of the Japanese — were crowded with smiling holiday makers, and made gay with devices of tinted tissue paper, dolphins, devils, dragons, and mythical winged creatures which at night amiably turned themselves into lanterns. Garlands of these, arranged close together, were stretched across the streets from ridgepole to ridgepole, and your jinrikisha whisked you through interminable arbors of soft illumination. The spectacle gave one an idea of fairyland, but then all Japan does that.

A land not like ours, that land of strange flowers,
Of dæmons and spooks with mysterious powers —
  Of gods who breathe ice, who cause peach-blooms and rice
And manage the moonshine and turn on the showers.

Each day has its fair or its festival there,
And life seems immune to all trouble and care —
  Perhaps only seems, in that island of dreams,
Sea-girdled and basking in magical air.

They 've streets of bazaars filled with lacquers and jars,
And silk stuffs, and sword-blades that tell of old wars;
  They 've Fuji's white cone looming up, bleak and lone,
As if it were trying to reach to the stars.

They 've temple and gongs, and grim Buddhas in throngs,
And pearl-powdered geisha with dances and songs:
  Each girl at her back has an imp, brown or black,
And dresses her hair in remarkable prongs.

On roadside and street toddling images meet,
And smirk and kotow in a way that is sweet;
  Their obis are tied with particular pride,
Their silken kimonos hang scant to the feet.

With purrs like a cat they all giggle and chat,
Now spreading their fans, and now holding them flat;
  A fan by its play whispers, "Go now!" or "Stay!"
"I hate you!" "I love you!"— a fan can say that!

Beneath a dwarf tree, here and there, two or three
Squat coolies are sipping small cups of green tea;
  They sputter, and leer, and cry out, and appear
Like bad little chessmen gone off on a spree.

At night — ah, at night the long streets are a sight,
With garlands of soft-colored lanterns alight —
  Blue, yellow, and red twinkling high overhead,
Like thousands of butterflies taking their flight.

Somewhere in the gloom that no lanterns illume
Stand groups of slim lilies and jonquils in bloom;
  On tiptoe, unseen 'mid a tangle of green,
They offer the midnight their cups of perfume.

At times, sweet and clear from some tea-garden near,
A ripple of laughter steals out to your ear;
  Anon the wind brings from a samisen's strings
The pathos that's born of a smile and a tear.

The difference between an English audience and a French audience at the theatre is marked. The Frenchman brings down a witticism on the wing. The Briton pauses for it to alight and give him reasonable time for deliberate aim. In English playhouses an appreciable number of seconds usually precede the smile or the ripple of laughter that follows a facetious turn of the least fineness. I disclaim all responsibility for this statement of my personal observation, since it has recently been indorsed by one of London's most eminent actors.

At the next table, taking his opal drops of absinthe, was a French gentleman with the *blasé* aspect of an empty champagne-bottle, which always has the air of saying: "I have lived!"

We often read of wonderful manifestations of memory, but they are always instances of the faculty working in some special direction. It is memory playing, like Paganini, on one string. No doubt the persons performing the phenomenal feats ascribed to them have forgotten more than they remember. To be able to repeat a hundred lines of verse after a single reading is no proof of a retentive mind, excepting so far as the hundred lines go. A man might easily fail under such a test, and yet have a good memory; by which I mean a catholic one, and that I imagine to be nearly the rarest of gifts. I have never met more than four or five persons possessing it. The small boy who defined memory as "the thing you forget with" described the faculty as it exists and works in the majority of men and women.

The survival in publishers of the imitative instinct is a strong argument in support of Mr. Darwin's theory of the descent of man. One publisher no sooner brings out a new style of book cover than half a dozen other publishers fall to duplicating it.

The cavalry sabre hung over the chimney-place with a knot of violets tied to the dinted guard, there being no known grave to decorate.

For many a year, on each Decoration Day, a sorrowful woman had come and fastened these flowers there. The first time she brought her offering she was a slender girl, as fresh as her own violets. It is a slender figure still, but there are threads of silver in the black hair.

FORTUNATE was Marcus Aurelius Antoninus, who in early youth was taught "to abstain from rhetoric, and poetry, and fine writing" — especially the fine writing. Simplicity is art's last word.

THE man is clearly an adventurer. In the seventeenth century he would have worn huge flint-lock pistols stuck into a wide leather belt, and been something in the seafaring line. The fellow is always smartly dressed, but where he lives and how he lives are as unknown as "what song the Sirens sang, or what name Achilles assumed when he hid himself among women." He is a man who apparently has no appointment with his breakfast and whose dinner is a chance acquaintance. His probable banker is the next person. A great city like this is the only geography for such a character. He would be impossible in a small country town, where everybody knows everybody and what everybody has for lunch.

I HAVE been seeking, thus far in vain, for the proprietor of the saying that "Economy is second or third cousin to Avarice." I went rather confidently to Rochefoucauld, but it is not among that gentleman's light luggage of cynical maxims.

THERE is a popular vague impression that butchers are not allowed to serve as jurors on murder trials. This is not really the case, but it logically might be. To a man daily familiar with the lurid incidents of the *abattoir*, the summary extinction of a fellow creature (whether the victim or the criminal) can scarcely seem a circumstance of so serious moment as to another man engaged in less strenuous pursuits.

WE do not, and cannot, read many of the novels that most delighted our ancestors. Some of our popular fiction is doubtless as poor, but poor with a difference. There is always a heavy demand for fresh mediocrity. In every generation the least cultivated taste has the largest appetite. There is ragtime literature as well as ragtime music for the many.

G—— is a man who had rather fail in a great purpose than not accomplish it in precisely his own way. He has the courage of his conviction and the intolerance of his courage. He is opposed to the death penalty for murder, but he would willingly have any one electrocuted who disagreed with him on the subject.

I HAVE thought of an essay to be called "On the Art of Short-Story Writing," but have given it up as smacking too much of the shop. It would be too *intime*, since I should have to deal chiefly with my own ways, and so give myself the false air of seeming to consider them of importance. It would interest nobody to know that I always write the last paragraph first, and then work directly up to that, avoiding all digressions and side issues. Then who on earth would care to be told about the trouble my characters cause me by talking too much? They *will* talk, and I have to let them; but when the story is finished, I go over the dialogue and strike out four fifths of the long speeches. I fancy that makes my characters pretty mad.

THIS is the golden age of the inventor. He is no longer looked upon as a madman or a wizard, incontinently to be made away with. Two or three centuries ago Marconi would not have escaped a ropeless end with his wireless telegraphy. Even so late as 1800, the friends of one Robert Fulton seriously entertained the luminous idea of hustling the poor man into an asylum for the unsound before he had a chance to fire up the boiler of his tiny steamboat on the Hudson River. In olden times the pillory and the whipping-post were among the gentler forms of encouragement awaiting the inventor. If a man devised an especially practical apple-peeler, he was in imminent danger of being peeled with it by an incensed populace. To-day we hail with enthusiasm a scientific or a mechanical discovery, and stand ready to make a stock company of it.

A MAN is known by the company his mind keeps. To live continually with noble books, with "high-erected thoughts seated in the heart of courtesy," teaches the soul good manners.

THE unconventional has ever a morbid attraction for a certain class of mind. There is always a small coterie of highly intellectual men and women eager to give welcome to whatever is eccentric, obscure, or chaotic. Worshipers at the shrine of the Unpopular, they tingle with a sense of tolerant superiority when they say: "Of course this is not the kind of thing *you* would like." Sometimes these impressionable souls almost seem to make a sort of reputation for their fetish.

I HEAR that B—— directed to have himself buried on the edge of the pond where his duck-stand was located, in order that flocks of migrating birds might fly over his grave every autumn. He did not have to die, to become a dead shot. A comrade once said of him: "Yes, B—— is a great sportsman. He has peppered everything from grouse in North Dakota to his best friend in the Maine woods."

WHEN the novelist introduces a bore into his novel he must not let him bore the reader. The fellow must be made amusing, which he would not be in real life. In nine cases out of ten an exact reproduction of real life would prove tedious. Facts are not necessarily valuable, and frequently they add nothing to fiction. The art of the realistic novelist sometimes seems akin to that of the Chinese tailor who perpetuated the old patch on the new trousers. True art selects and paraphrases, but seldom gives a verbatim translation.

THE last meeting I had with Lowell was in the north room of his house at Elmwood, the sleeping-room I had occupied during a two years' tenancy of the place in his absence abroad. He was lying half propped up in bed, convalescing from one of the severe attacks that were ultimately to prove fatal. Near the bed was a chair on which stood a marine picture in aquarelle — a stretch of calm sea, a bit of rocky shore in the foreground, if I remember, and a vessel at anchor. The afternoon sunlight, falling through the window, cast a bloom over the picture, which was turned toward Lowell. From time to time, as he spoke, his eyes rested thoughtfully on the water-color. A friend, he said, had just sent it to him. It seemed to me then, and the fancy has often haunted me since, that that ship, in the golden haze, with topsails loosened, was waiting to bear his spirit away.

Civilization is the lamb's skin in which barbarism masquerades. If somebody has already said that, I forgive him the mortification he causes me. At the beginning of the twentieth century barbarism can throw off its gentle disguise, and burn a man at the stake as complacently as in the Middle Ages.

What is slang in one age sometimes goes into the vocabulary of the purist in the next. On the other hand, expressions that once were not considered inelegant are looked at askance in the period following. The word "brass" was formerly an accepted synonym for money; but at present, when it takes on that significance, it is not admitted into genteel circles of language. It may be said to have seen better days, like another word I have in mind — a word that has become slang, employed in the sense which once did not exclude it from very good society. A friend lately informed me that he had "fired" his housekeeper — that is, dismissed her. He little dreamed that he was speaking excellent Elizabethan.

THE "Journal des Goncourt" is crowded with beautiful and hideous things, like a Japanese museum.

"AND *s*he *s*huddered a*s* *s*he *s*at, *s*till *s*ilent, on her *s*eat, and he *s*aw that *s*he *s*huddered." This is from Anthony Trollope's novel, "Can You Forgive Her?" Can you forgive him? is the next question.

A LITTLE thing may be perfect, but perfection is not a little thing. Possessing this quality, a trifle "no bigger than an agate stone on the forefinger of an alderman" shall outlast the Pyramids. The world will have forgotten all the great masterpieces of literature when it forgets Lovelace's three verses to Lucasta on his going to the wars. More durable than marble or bronze are the words, "I could not love thee, deare, so much, loved I not honour more."

I CALLED on the dear old doctor this afternoon to say good-by. I shall probably not find him here when I come back from the long voyage which I have in front of me. He is very fragile, and looks as though a puff of wind would blow him away. He said himself, with his old-time cheerfulness, that he was attached to this earth by only a little piece of twine. He has perceptibly failed since I saw him a month ago; but he was full of the wise and radiant talk to which all the world has listened, and will miss. I found him absorbed in a newly-made card-catalogue of his library. "It was absurd of me to have it done," he remarked. "What I really require is a little bookcase holding only two volumes; then I could go from one to the other in alternation and always find each book as fresh as if I never had read it." This arraignment of his memory was in pure jest, for the doctor's mind was to the end like an unclouded crystal. It was interesting to note how he studied himself, taking his own pulse, as it were, and diagnosing his own case in a sort of scientific, impersonal way, as if it were somebody else's case and he were the consulting specialist. I intended to spend a quarter of an hour with him, and he kept me three hours. I went there rather depressed, but I returned home leavened with his good spirits, which, I think, will never desert him, here or hereafter. To keep the heart unwrinkled, to be hopeful, kindly, cheerful, reverent — that is to triumph over old age.

THE thing one reads and likes, and then forgets, is of no account. The thing that stays, and haunts one, and refuses to be forgotten, that is the sincere thing. I am describing the impression left upon me by Mr. Howells's blank-verse sketch called "Father and Mother: a Mystery" — a strangely touching and imaginative piece of work, not unlike in effect to some of Maeterlinck's psychical dramas. As I read on, I seemed to be standing in a shadow cast by some half-remembered experience of my own in a previous state of existence. When I went to bed that night I had to lie awake and think it over as an event that had actually befallen me. I should call the effect *weird*, if the word had not lately been worked to death. The gloom of Poe and the spirituality of Hawthorne touch cold finger-tips in those three or four pages.

For a character-study — a man made up entirely of limitations. His conservatism and negative qualities to be represented as causing him to attain success where men of conviction and real ability fail of it.

A dark, saturnine man sat opposite me at table on board the steamer. During the entire run from Sandy Hook to Fastnet Light he addressed no one at meal-times excepting his table steward. Seated next to him, on the right, was a vivacious gentleman, who, like Gratiano, in the play, spoke "an infinite deal of nothing." He made persistent and pathetic attempts to lure his silent neighbor (we had christened him "William the Silent") into conversation, but a monosyllable was always the poor result — until one day. It was the last day of the voyage. We had stopped at the entrance to Queenstown harbor to deliver the mails, and some fish had been brought aboard. The vivacious gentleman was in a high state of excitement that morning at table. "Fresh fish!" he exclaimed; "actually fresh! They seem quite different from ours. Irish fish, of course. Can you tell me, sir," he inquired, turning to his gloomy shipmate, "what *kind* of fish these are?" "Cork soles," said the saturnine man, in a deep voice, and then went on with his breakfast.

Lowell used to find food for great mirth in General George P. Morris's line,

> Her heart and morning broke together.

Lowell's well-beloved Dr. Donne, however, had an attack of the same platitude, and possibly inoculated poor Morris. Even literature seems to have its mischief-making bacilli. The late "incomparable and ingenious Dean of St. Paul's" says,

> The day breaks not, it is my heart.

I think Dr. Donne's case rather worse than Morris's. Chaucer had the malady in a milder form when he wrote:

> Up roos the sonne, and up roos Emelye.

The charming naïveté of it!

Sitting in Ellen Terry's dressing-room at the Lyceum Theatre one evening during that lady's temporary absence on the stage, Sarah Bernhardt picked up a crayon and wrote this pretty word on the mirror — *Dearling*, — mistaking it for the word darling. The French actress lighted by chance upon a Spenserianism now become obsolete without good reason. It is a more charming adjective than the one that has replaced it.

A DEAD author appears to be bereft of all earthly rights. He is scarcely buried before old magazines and newspapers are ransacked in search of matters which, for reason sufficient to him, he had carefully excluded from the definitive edition of his collected writings.

> He gave the people of his best;
> His worst he kept, his best he gave.

One can imagine a poet tempted to address some such appeal as this to any possible future publisher of his poems:

> Take what thou wilt, a lyric or a line,
> Take all, take nothing — and God send thee cheer!
> But my anathema on thee and thine
> If thou add'st aught to what is printed here.

THE claim of this country to call itself "The Land of the Free" must be held in abeyance until every man in it, whether he belongs or does not belong to a labor organization, shall have the right to work for his daily bread.

THERE is a strain of primitive poetry running through the entire Irish race, a fleeting lyrical emotion which expresses itself in a flash, usually in connection with love of country and kindred across the sea. I had a touching illustration of it the other morning. The despot who reigns over our kitchen was gathering a mess of dandelions on the rear lawn. It was one of those blue and gold days which seem especially to belong to New England. "It 's in County Westmeath I 'd be this day," she said, looking up at me. "*I'd go cool my hands in the grass on my ould mother's grave in the bit of churchyard foreninst the priest's house at Mullingar.*" I have seen poorer poetry than that in the magazines.

Speaking of the late Major Pond, the well-known director of a lecture bureau, an old client of his remarked: "He was a most capable manager, but it always made me a little sore to have him deduct twenty-five per cent commission." "Pond's Extract," murmured one of the gentlemen present.

Each of our great towns has its "Little Italy," with shops where nothing is spoken but Italian and streets in which the alien pedestrian had better not linger after nightfall. The chief industry of these exotic communities seems to be spaghetti and stilettos. What with our Little Italys and Chinatowns, and the like, an American need not cross the ocean in order to visit foreign lands and enjoy the benefits of older civilizations.

Poets are made as well as born, the proverb notwithstanding. They are made possible by the general love of poetry and the consequent imperious demand for it. When this is non-existent, poets become mute, the atmosphere stifles them. There would have been no Shakespeare had there been no Elizabethan audience. That was an age when, as Emerson finely puts it,

> Men became
> Poets, for the air was fame.

THE stolid gentleman in livery who has his carriage-stand at the corner opposite my house is constantly touching on the extremes of human experience, with probably not the remotest perception of the fact. Now he takes a pair of lovers out for an airing, and now he drives the absconding bank-teller to the railway station. Excepting as question of distance, the man has positively no choice between a theatre and a graveyard. I met him this morning dashing up to the portals of Trinity Church with a bridal party, and this afternoon, as I was crossing Cambridge Bridge, I saw him creeping along next to the hearse, on his way to Mount Auburn. The wedding afforded him no pleasure, and the funeral gave him no grief; yet he was a factor in both. It is his odd destiny to be wholly detached from the vital part of his own acts. If the carriage itself could speak! The autobiography of a public hack written without reservation would be dramatic reading.

In this blotted memorandum-book are a score or two of suggestions for essays, sketches, and poems, which I have not written, and never shall write. The instant I jot down an idea the desire to utilize it leaves me, and I turn away to do something unpremeditated. The shabby volume has become a sort of Potter's Field where I bury my literary intentions, good and bad, without any belief in their final resurrection.

A Stage-direction: *Exit Time; enter Eternity — with a soliloquy.*

ASIDES

TOM FOLIO

In my early Boston days a gentle soul was often to be met with about town, furtively haunting old book-shops and dusty editorial rooms, a man of ingratiating simplicity of manner, who always spoke in a low, hesitating voice, with a note of refinement in it. He was a devout worshiper of Elia, and wrote pleasant discursive essays smacking somewhat of his master's flavor — suggesting rather than imitating it — which he signed "Tom Folio." I forget how he glided into my acquaintanceship; doubtless in some way too shy and elusive for remembrance. I never knew him intimately, perhaps no one did, but the intercourse between us was most cordial, and our chance meetings and bookish chats extended over a space of a dozen years.

Tom Folio — I cling to the winning pseudonym — was sparely built and under medium height, or maybe a slight droop of the shoulders made it seem so, with a fragile look about him and an aspect of youth that was not his. Encountering him casually on a street corner, you would, at the first glance, have taken him for a youngish man, but the second glance left you doubtful. It was a figure that struck a note of singularity and would have attracted your attention even in a crowd.

During the first four or five years of our acquaintance, meeting him only out of doors or in shops, I had never happened to see him with his hat off. One day he recklessly removed it, and in the twinkling of an eye he became an elderly bald-headed man. The Tom Folio I once knew had virtually vanished. An instant earlier he was a familiar shape; an instant later, an almost unrecognizable individual. A narrow fringe of light-colored hair, extending from ear to ear under the rear brim of his hat, had perpetrated an unintentional deception by leading one to suppose a head profusely covered with curly locks. "Tom Folio," I said, "put on your hat and come back!" But after that day he never seemed young to me.

I had few or no inklings of his life disconnected with the streets and the book-stalls, chiefly those on Cornhill or in the vicinity. It is possible I am wrong in inferring that he occupied a room somewhere at the South End or in South Boston, and lived entirely alone, heating his coffee and boiling his egg over an alcohol lamp. I got from him one or two fortuitous hints of quaint housekeeping. Every winter, it appeared, some relative, far or near, sent him a large batch of mince pies, twenty or thirty at least. He once spoke to me of having laid in his winter pie, just as another might speak of laying in his winter coal. The only fireside companion Tom Folio ever alluded to in my presence was a Maltese cat, whose poor health seriously disturbed him from time to time. I suspected those mince pies. The cat, I recollect, was named Miss Mowcher.

If he had any immediate family ties beyond this I was unaware of them, and not curious to be enlightened on the subject. He was more picturesque solitary. I preferred him to remain so. Other figures introduced into the background of the canvas would have spoiled the artistic effect.

Tom Folio was a cheerful, lonely man — a recluse even when he allowed himself to be jostled and hurried along on the turbulent stream of humanity sweeping in opposite directions through Washington Street and its busy estuaries. He was in the crowd, but not of it. I had so little real knowledge of him that I was obliged to imagine his more intimate environments. However wide of the mark my conjectures may have fallen, they were as satisfying to me as facts would have been. His secluded room I could picture to myself with a sense of certainty — the couch (a sofa by day), the cupboard, the writing-table with its student lamp, the litter of pamphlets and old quartos and octavos in tattered bindings, among which were scarce reprints of his beloved Charles Lamb, and perhaps — nay, surely — an *editio princeps* of the "Essays."

The gentle Elia never had a gentler follower or a more loving disciple than Tom Folio. He moved and had much of his being in the early part of the last century. To him the South-Sea House was the most important edifice on the globe, remaining the same venerable pile it used to be, in spite of all the changes that had befallen it. It was there Charles Lamb passed the novitiate of his long years of clerkship in the East India Company. In Tom Folio's fancy a slender, boyish figure was still seated, quill in hand, behind those stately porticoes looking upon Threadneedle Street and Bishopsgate. That famous first paper in the "Essays," describing the South-Sea House and the group of human oddities which occupied desks within its gloomy chambers, had left an indelible impression upon the dreamer. Every line traced by the "lean annuitant" was as familiar to Tom Folio as if he had written it himself. Stray scraps, which had escaped the vigilance of able editors, were known to him, and it was his to unearth amid a heap of mouldy, worm-eaten magazines, a handful of leaves hitherto forgotten of all men. Trifles, yes — but Charles Lamb's! "The king's chaff is as good as other people's corn," says Tom Folio.

Often his talk was sweet and racy with old-fashioned phrases; the talk of a man who loved books and drew habitual breath in an atmosphere of fine thought. Next to Charles Lamb, but at a convenable distance, Izaak Walton was Tom Folio's favorite. His poet was Alexander Pope, though he thought Mr. Addison's tragedy of "Cato" contained some proper good lines. Our friend was a wide reader in English classics, greatly preferring the literature of the earlier periods to that of the Victorian age. His smiling, tenderly expressed disapprobation of various modern authors was enchanting. John Keats's verses were monstrous pretty, but over-ornamented. A little too much lucent syrup tinct with cinnamon, don't you think? The poetry of Shelley might have been composed in the moon by a slightly deranged, well-meaning person. If you wanted a sound mind in a sound metrical body, why there was Mr. Pope's "Essay on Man." There was something winsome and bygone in the general make-up of Tom Folio. No man living in the world ever seemed to me to live so much out of it, or to live more comfortably.

At times I half suspected him of a convalescent amatory disappointment. Perhaps long before I knew him he had taken a little sentimental journey, the unsuccessful end of which had touched him with a gentle sadness. It was something far off and softened by memory. If Tom Folio had any love affair on hand in my day, it must have been of an airy, platonic sort —a chaste secret passion for Mistress Peg Woffington or Nell Gwyn, or possibly Mr. Waller's Saccharissa.

Although Tom Folio was not a collector — that means dividends and bank balances — he had a passion for the Past and all its belongings, with a virtuoso's knowledge of them. A fan painted by Vanloo, a bit of rare Nankin (he had caught from Charles Lamb the love of old china), or an undoctored stipple of Bartolozzi, gave him delight in the handling, though he might not aspire to ownership. I believe he would willingly have drunk any horrible decoction from a silver teapot of Queen Anne's time. These things were not for him in a coarse, materialistic sense; in a spiritual sense he held possession of them in fee-simple. I learned thus much of his tastes one day during an hour we spent together in the rear showroom of a dealer in antiquities.

I have spoken of Tom Folio as lonely, but I am inclined to think that I misstated it. He had hosts of friends who used to climb the rather steep staircase leading to that modest third-story front room which I have imagined for him — a room with Turkey-red curtains, I like to believe, and a rare engraving of a scene from Mr. Hogarth's excellent moral of "The Industrious and Idle Apprentices" pinned against the chimney breast. Young Chatterton, who was not always the best of company, dropped in at intervals. There Mr. Samuel Pepys had a special chair reserved for him by the window, where he could catch a glimpse of the pretty housemaid over the way, chatting with the policeman at the area railing. Dr. Johnson and the unworldly author of "The Deserted Village" were frequent visitors, sometimes appearing together arm-in-arm, with James Boswell, Esq., of Auchinleck, following obsequiously behind. Not that Tom Folio did not have callers vastly more aristocratic, though he could have had none pleasanter or wholesomer. Sir Philip Sidney (who must have given Folio that copy of the "Arcadia"), the Viscount St. Albans, and even two or three others before whom either of these might have doffed his bonnet, did not disdain to gather round that hearthstone. Fielding, Smollett, Sterne, Defoe, Dick Steele, Dean Swift — there was no end to them! On certain nights, when all the stolid neighborhood was lapped in slumber, the narrow street stretching beneath Tom Folio's windows must have been blocked with invisible coaches and sedan-chairs, and illuminated by the visionary glare of torches borne by shadowy linkboys hurrying hither and thither. A man so sought after and companioned cannot be described as lonely.

My memory here recalls the fact that he had a few friends less insubstantial — that quaint anatomy perched on the top of a hand-organ, to whom Tom Folio was wont to give a bite of his apple; and the brown-legged little Neapolitan who was always nearly certain of a copper when this multi-millionaire strolled through the slums on a Saturday afternoon — Saturday probably being the essayist's pay-day. The withered woman of the peanut-stand on the corner over against Faneuil Hall Market knew him for a friend, as did also the blind lead-pencil merchant, whom Tom Folio, on occasions, safely piloted across the stormy traffic of Dock Square. *Noblesse oblige!* He was no stranger in those purlieus. Without designing to confuse small things with great, I may say that a certain strip of pavement in North Street could be pointed out as Tom Folio's Walk, just as Addison's Walk is pointed out on the banks of the Cherwell at Oxford.

I used to observe that when Tom Folio was

not in quest of a print or a pamphlet or some such urgent thing, but was walking for mere recreation, he instinctively avoided respectable latitudes. He liked best the squalid, ill-kept thoroughfares shadowed by tall, smudgy tenement-houses and teeming with unprosperous, noisy life. Perhaps he had, half consciously, a sense of subtle kinship to the unsuccess and cheerful resignation of it all.

Returning home from abroad one October morning several years ago, I was told that that simple spirit had passed on. His death had been little heeded; but in him had passed away an intangible genuine bit of Old Boston — as genuine a bit, in its kind, as the Autocrat himself — a personality not to be restored or replaced. Tom Folio could never happen again!

Strolling to-day through the streets of the older section of the town, I miss many a venerable landmark submerged in the rising tide of change, but I miss nothing quite so much as I do the sight of Tom Folio entering the doorway of the Old Corner Bookstore, or carefully taking down a musty volume from its shelf at some melancholy old book-stall on Cornhill.

FLEABODY AND OTHER QUEER NAMES

When an English novelist does us the honor to introduce any of our countrymen into his fiction, he generally displays a commendable desire to present something typical in the way of names for his adopted characters — to give a dash of local color, as it were, with his nomenclature. His success is seldom commensurate to the desire. He falls into the error of appealing to his invention, instead of consulting some city directory, in which he would find more material than he could exhaust in ten centuries. Charles Reade might have secured in the pages of such a compendium a happier title than Fullalove for his Yankee sea-captain; though I doubt, on the whole, if Anthony Trollope could have discovered anything better than Olivia Q. Fleabody for the young woman from "the States" in his novel called "Is He Popenjoy?"

To christen a sprightly young female advocate of woman's rights Olivia Q. Fleabody was very happy indeed; to be candid, it was much better than was usual with Mr. Trollope, whose understanding of American life and manners was not enlarged by extensive travel in this country. An English tourist's preconceived idea of us is a thing he brings over with him on the steamer and carries home again intact; it is as much a part of his indispensable impedimenta as his hat-box. But Fleabody is excellent; it was probably suggested by Peabody, which may have struck Mr. Trollope as comical (just as Trollope strikes *us* as comical), or, at least, as not serious. What a capital name Veronica Trollope would be for a hoydenish young woman in a society novel! I fancy that all foreign names are odd to the alien. I remember that the signs above shop doors in England and on the Continent used to amuse me often enough, when I was over there. It is a notable circumstance that extraordinary names never seem extraordinary to the persons bearing them. If a fellow-creature were branded Ebenezer Cuttlefish, he would remain to the end of his days quite unconscious of anything out of the common.

I am aware that many of our American names are sufficiently queer; but English writers make merry over them, as if our most eccentric were not thrown into the shade by some of their own. No American, living or dead, can surpass the verbal infelicity of Knatchbull-Hugessen, for example — if the gentleman will forgive me for conscripting him. Quite as remarkable, in a grimly significant way, is the appellation of a British officer who was fighting the Boers in the Transvaal in the year of blessed memory 1899. This young soldier, who highly distinguished himself on the field, was known to his brothers-in-arms as Major Pine Coffin. I trust that the gallant major became a colonel later and is still alive. It would eclipse the gayety of nations to lose a man with a name like that.

Several years ago I read in the sober police reports of the "Pall Mall Gazette" an account of a young man named George F. Onions, who was arrested (it ought to have been by "a peeler") for purloining money from his employers, Messrs. Joseph Pickles & Son, stuff merchants, of Bradford — *des noms bien idylliques!* What mortal could have a more ludicrous name than Onions, unless it were Pickles, or Pickled Onions? And then for Onions to rob Pickles! Could there be a more incredible coincidence? As a coincidence it is nearly sublime. No story-writer would dare to present that fact or those names in his fiction; neither would be accepted as possible. Meanwhile Olivia Q. Fleabody is *ben trovato.*

A NOTE ON "L'AIGLON"

THE night scene on the battlefield of Wagram in "L'Aiglon"—an episode whose sharp pathos pierces the heart and the imagination like the point of a rapier — bears a striking resemblance to a picturesque passage in Victor Hugo's "Les Misérables." It is the one intense great moment in the play, and has been widely discussed, but so far as I am aware none of M. Rostand's innumerable critics has touched on the resemblance mentioned. In the master's romance it is not the field of Wagram, but the field of Waterloo, that is magically repeopled with contending armies of spooks, to use the grim old Dutch word, and made vivid to the mind's eye. The passage occurs at the end of the sixteenth chapter in the second part of "Les Misérables" (Cosette), and runs as follows:

"Le champ de Waterloo aujourd'hui a le calme qui appartient à la terre, support impassible de l'homme, et il resemble à toutes les plaines. La nuit pourtant une espèce de brume visionnaire s'en dégage, et si quelque voyageur s'y promène, s'il regarde, s'il écoute, s'il rêve comme Virgile dans les funestes plaines de Philippes, l'hallucination de la catastrophe le saisit. L'effrayant 18 juin revit; la fausse colline-monument s'efface, ce lion quelconque se dissipe, le champ de bataille reprend sa réalité; des lignes d'infanterie ondulent dans la plaine, des galops furieux traversent l'horizon; le songeur effaré voit l'éclair des sabres, l'étincelle des bayonnettes, le flamboiement des bombes, l'entre-croisement monstrueux des tonnerres; il entend, comme un râle au fond d'une tombe, la clameur vague de la bataille-fantôme; ces ombres, ce sont les grenadiers; ces lueurs, ce sont les cuirassiers; . . . tout cela n'est plus et se heurte et combat encore; et les ravins s'empourprent, et les arbres frissonnent, et il y a de la furie jusque dans les nuées, et, dans les ténèbres, toutes ces hauteurs farouches, Mont-Saint-Jean, Hougomont, Frischemont, Papelotte, Plancenoit, apparaissent confusément couronnées de tourbillons de spectres s'exterminant." [1]

[1] The field of Waterloo has to-day the peacefulness which belongs to earth, the impassive support of man, and is like all other plains. At night, however, a kind of visionary mist is exhaled, and if any traveler walks there, and watches and listens, and dreams like Virgil on the sorrowful plains of Phi-

Here is the whole battle scene in "L'Aiglon," with scarcely a gruesome detail omitted. The vast plain glimmering in phantasmal light; the ghostly squadrons hurling themselves against one another (seen only through the eyes of the poor little Duke of Reichstadt); the mangled shapes lying motionless in various postures of death upon the blood-stained sward; the moans of the wounded rising up and sweeping by like vague wailings of the wind — all this might be taken for an artful appropriation of Victor Hugo's text; but I do not think it was, though it is possible that a faint reflection of a brilliant page, read in early youth, still lingered on the retina of M. Rostand's memory. If such were the case, it does not necessarily detract from the

lippi, the hallucination of the catastrophe takes possession of him. The terrible June 18 relives; the artificial commemorative mound effaces itself, the lion disappears, the field of battle assumes its reality; lines of infantry waver on the plain, the horizon is broken by furious charges of cavalry; the alarmed dreamer sees the gleam of sabres, the glimmer of bayonets, the lurid glare of bursting shells, the clashing of mighty thunderbolts; the muffled clamor of the phantom conflict comes to him like dying moans from the tomb; these shadows are grenadiers, these lights are cuirassiers . . . all this does not really exist, yet the combat goes on; the ravines are stained with purple, the trees tremble, there is fury even in the clouds, and in the obscurity the sombre heights — Mont-Saint-Jean, Hougomont, Frischemont, Papelotte, and Plancenoit — appear dimly crowned with throngs of apparitions annihilating one another.

integrity of the conception or the playwright's presentment of it.

The idea of repeopling old battlefields with the shades of vanished hosts is not novel. In such tragic spots the twilight always lays a dark hand on the imagination, and prompts one to invoke the unappeased spirit of the past that haunts the place. One summer evening long ago, as I was standing alone by the ruined walls of Hougomont, with that sense of not being alone which is sometimes so strangely stirred by solitude, I had a sudden vision of that desperate last charge of Napoleon's Old Guard. Marshal Ney rose from the grave and again shouted those heroic words to Drouet d'Erlon: "Are you not going to get yourself killed?" For an instant a thousand sabres flashed in the air. The deathly silence that accompanied the ghostly onset was an added poignancy to the short-lived dream. A moment later I beheld a hunched little figure mounted on a white horse with housings of purple velvet. The reins lay slack in the rider's hand; his three-cornered hat was slouched over his brows, and his chin rested on the breast of his greatcoat. Thus he slowly rode away through the twilight, and nobody cried, *Vive l'Empereur!*

The ground on which a famous battle has been fought casts a spell upon every man's mind; and the impression made upon two men of poetic genius, like Victor Hugo and Edmond Rostand, might well be nearly identical. This sufficiently explains the likeness between the fantastic silhouette in "Les Misérables" and the battle of the ghosts in "L'Aiglon." A muse so rich in the improbable as M. Rostand's need not borrow a piece of supernaturalness from anybody.

PLOT AND CHARACTER

HENRY JAMES, in his paper on Anthony Trollope, says that if Trollope "had taken sides on the rather superficial opposition between novels of character and novels of plot, I can imagine him to have said (except that he never expressed himself in epigram) that he preferred the former class, inasmuch as character in itself is plot, while plot is by no means character." So neat an antithesis would surely never have found itself between Mr. Trollope's lips if Mr. James had not cunningly lent it to him. Whatever theory of novel-writing Mr. Trollope may have preached, his almost invariable practice was to have a plot. He always had a *story* to tell, and a story involves beginning, middle, and end—in short, a framework of some description.

There have been delightful books filled wholly with character-drawing, but they have not been great novels. The great novel deals with human action as well as with mental portraiture and analysis. That "character in itself is plot" is true only in a limited sense. A plan, a motive with a logical conclusion, is as necessary to a novel or a romance as it is to a drama. A group of skillfully made-up men and women lounging in the green room or at the wings is not the play. It is not enough to say that this is Romeo and that Lady Macbeth. It is not enough to inform us that certain passions are supposed to be embodied in such and such persons: these persons should be placed in situations developing those passions. A series of unrelated scenes and dialogues leading to nothing is inadequate.

Mr. James's engaging epigram seems to me vulnerable at both ends — unlike Achilles. "Plot is by no means character." Strictly speaking, it is not. It appears to me, however, that plot approaches nearer to being character than character does to being plot. Plot necessitates action, and it is impossible to describe a man's actions, under whatever conditions, without revealing something of his character, his way of looking at things, his moral and mental pose. What a hero of fiction *does* paints him better than what he *says*, and vastly better than anything his creator may say of him. Mr. James asserts that "we care what happens to people only in proportion as we know what people are." I think we care very little what people are (in fiction) when we do not know what happens to them.

THE CRUELTY OF SCIENCE

In the process of their experiments upon the bodies of living animals some anatomists do not, I fear, sufficiently realize that

> The poor beetle, that we tread upon,
> In corporal sufferance, finds a pang as great
> As when a giant dies.

I am not for a moment challenging the necessity of vivisection, though distinguished surgeons have themselves challenged it ; I merely contend that science is apt to be cold-hearted ; and does not seem always to take into consideration the tortures she inflicts in her search for knowledge.

Just now, in turning over the leaves of an old number of the "London Lancet," I came upon the report of a lecture on experimental physiology delivered by Professor William Rutherford before a learned association in London. Though the type had become antiquated and the paper yellowed in the lapse of years, the pathos of those pages was alive and palpitating.

The following passages from the report will illustrate not unfairly the point I am making.

In the course of his remarks the lecturer exhibited certain interesting experiments on living frogs. Intellectually I go very strongly for Professor Rutherford, but I am bound to confess that the weight of my sympathy rests with the frogs.

"Observe this frog [said the professor], it is regarding our manœuvres with a somewhat lively air. Now and then it gives a jump. What the precise object of its leaps may be I dare not pretend to say; but probably it regards us with some apprehension, and desires to escape."

To be perfectly impartial, it must be admitted that the frog had some slight reason for apprehension. The lecturer proceeded:—

"I touch one of its toes, and you see it resents the molestation in a very decided manner. Why does it so struggle to get away when I pinch its toes? Doubtless, you will say, because it feels the pinch and would rather not have it repeated. I now behead the animal with the aid of a sharp chisel. . . . The headless trunk lies as though it were dead. The spinal cord seems to be suffering from shock. Probably, however, it will soon recover from this. . . . Observe that the animal has now *spontaneously* drawn up its legs and arms, and it is sitting with its neck erect just as if it had not lost its head at all. I pinch its toes, and you see the leg is at once thrust out as if to spurn away the offending instrument. Does it still feel? and is the motion still the result of the volition?"

That the frog did feel, and delicately hinted at the circumstance, there seems to be no room to doubt, for Professor Rutherford related that having once decapitated a frog, the animal suddenly bounded from the table, a movement that presumably indicated a kind of consciousness. He then returned to the subject immediately under observation, pinched its foot again, the frog again "resenting the stimulation." He then thrust a needle down the spinal cord. "The limbs are now flaccid," observed the experimenter; "we may wait as long as we please, but a pinch of the toes will never again cause the limbs of this animal to move." Here is where congratulations can come in for *la grenouille.* That frog being concluded, the lecturer continued: —

"I take another frog. In this case I open the cranium and remove the brain and medulla oblongata. . . . I thrust a pin through the nose and hang the animal thereby to a support, so that it can move its pendent legs without any difficulty. . . . I gently pinch the toes. . . . The leg of the same side is pulled up. . . . I pinch the same more severely. . . . Both legs are thrown into motion."

Having thus satisfactorily proved that the wretched creature could still suffer acutely, the professor resumed: —

"The cutaneous nerves of the frog are extremely sensitive to acids; so I put a drop of acetic acid on the outside of one knee. This, you see, gives rise to most violent movements both of arms and legs, and notice particularly that the animal is using the toes of the leg on the same side for the purpose of rubbing the irritated spot. I dip the whole animal into water in order to wash away the acid, and now it is all at rest again. . . . I put a drop of acid on the skin over the lumbar region of the spine. . . . Both feet are instantly raised to the irritated spot. The animal is able to localize the seat of irritation. . . . I wash the acid from the back, and I amputate one of the feet at the ankle. . . . I apply a drop of acid over the knee of the footless leg. . . . Again, the animal turns the leg towards the knee, as if to reach the irritated spot with the toes; these, however, are not now available. But watch the other foot. The *foot of the other leg* is now being used to rub away the acid. The animal, finding that the object is not accomplished with the foot of the same side, uses the other one."

I think that at least one thing will be patent to every unprejudiced reader of these excerpts, namely — that any frog (with its head on or its head off) which happened to make the personal acquaintance of Professor Rutherford must have found him poor company. What benefit science may have derived from such association I am not qualified to pronounce upon. The lecturer showed conclusively that the frog is a peculiarly sensitive and intelligent little batrachian. I hope that the genial professor, in the years which followed, did not frequently consider it necessary to demonstrate the fact.

LEIGH HUNT AND BARRY CORNWALL

IT has recently become the fashion to speak disparagingly of Leigh Hunt as a poet, to class him as a sort of pursuivant or shield-bearer to Coleridge, Shelley, and Keats. Truth to tell, Hunt was not a Keats nor a Shelley nor a Coleridge, but he was a most excellent Hunt. He was a delightful essayist—quite unsurpassed, indeed, in his blithe, optimistic way — and as a poet deserves to rank high among the lesser singers of his time. I should place him far above Barry Cornwall, who has not half the freshness, variety, and originality of his compeer.

I instance Barry Cornwall because there has seemed a disposition since his death to praise him unduly. Barry Cornwall has always struck me as extremely artificial, especially in his dramatic sketches. His verses in this line are mostly soft Elizabethan echoes. Of course a dramatist may find it to his profit to go out of his own age and atmosphere for inspiration; but in order successfully to do so he must be a dramatist. Barry Cornwall fell short of filling the rôle; he got no farther than the composing of brief disconnected scenes and scraps of soliloquies, and a tragedy entitled "Mirandola," for which the stage had no use. His chief claim to recognition lies in his lyrics. Here, as in the dramatic studies, his attitude is nearly always affected. He studiously strives to reproduce the form and spirit of the early poets. Being a Londoner, he naturally sings much of rural English life, but his England is the England of two or three centuries ago. He has a great deal to say about the "falcon," but the poor bird has the air of beating fatigued wings against the book-shelves of a well-furnished library. This well-furnished library was — if I may be pardoned a mixed image — the rock on which Barry Cornwall split. He did not look into his own heart, and write: he looked into his books.

A poet need not confine himself to his individual experiences; the world is all before him where to choose; but there are subjects which he had better not handle unless he have some personal knowledge of them. The sea is one of these. The man who sang,

> The sea! the sea! the open sea!
> The blue, the fresh, *the ever free!*

(a couplet which the gifted Hopkins might have penned), should never have permitted himself to

The angel wrote, and vanish'd. The next night
It came again with a great wakening light
And show'd the names whom love of God had bless'd,
And lo! Ben Adhem's name led all the rest.

Leigh Hunt

sing of the ocean. I am quoting from one of Barry Cornwall's most popular lyrics. When I first read this singularly vapid poem years ago, in mid-Atlantic, I wondered if the author had ever laid eyes on any piece of water wider than the Thames at Greenwich, and in looking over Barry Cornwall's "Life and Letters" I am not so much surprised as amused to learn that he was never out of sight of land in the whole course of his existence. It is to be said of him more positively than the captain of the Pinafore said it of himself, that he was hardly ever sick at sea.

Imagine Byron or Shelley, who knew the ocean in all its protean moods, piping such thin feebleness as —

> The blue, the fresh, the ever free!

To do that required a man whose acquaintance with the deep was limited to a view of it from an upper window at Margate or Scarborough. Even frequent dinners of turbot and whitebait at the sign of The Ship and Turtle will not enable one to write sea poetry.

Considering the actual facts, there is something weird in the statement,

> I 'm on the sea! I 'm on the sea!
> I am where I would ever be.

The words, to be sure, are placed in the mouth of an imagined sailor, but they are none the less diverting. The stanza containing the distich ends with a striking piece of realism:

> If a storm should come and awake the deep,
> What matter? I shall ride and sleep.

This is the course of action usually pursued by sailors during a gale. The first or second mate goes around and tucks them up comfortably, each in his hammock, and serves them out an extra ration of grog after the storm is over.

Barry Cornwall must have had an exceptionally winning personality, for he drew to him the friendship of men as differently constituted as Thackeray, Carlyle, Browning, and Forster. He was liked by the best of his time, from Charles Lamb down to Algernon Swinburne, who caught a glimpse of the aged poet in his vanishing. The personal magnetism of an author does not extend far beyond the orbit of his contemporaries. It is of the lyrist and not of the man I am speaking here. One could wish he had written more prose like his admirable "Recollections of Elia."

Barry Cornwall seldom sounds a natural note, but when he does it is extremely sweet. That little ballad in the minor key beginning,

> Touch us gently, Time!
> Let us glide adown thy stream,

was written in one of his rare moments. Leigh Hunt, though not without questionable mannerisms, was rich in the inspiration that came but infrequently to his friend. Hunt's verse is full of natural felicities. He also was a bookman, but, unlike Barry Cornwall, he generally knew how to mint his gathered gold, and to stamp the coinage with his own head. In "Hero and Leander," there is one line which, at my valuing, is worth any twenty stanzas that Barry Cornwall has written:

So might they now have lived, and so have died;
The story's heart, to me, still beats against its side.

Hunt's fortunate verse about the kiss Jane Carlyle gave him lingers on everybody's lip. That and the rhyme of "Abou Ben Adhem and the Angel" are spice enough to embalm a man's memory. After all, it takes only a handful.

DECORATION DAY

How quickly Nature takes possession of a deserted battlefield, and goes to work repairing the ravages of man! With invisible magic hand she smooths the rough earthworks, fills the rifle-pits with delicate flowers, and wraps the splintered tree-trunks with her fluent drapery of tendrils. Soon the whole sharp outline of the spot is lost in unremembering grass. Where the deadly rifle-ball whistled through the foliage, the robin or the thrush pipes its tremulous note; and where the menacing shell described its curve through the air, a harmless crow flies in circles. Season after season the gentle work goes on, healing the wounds and rents made by the merciless enginery of war, until at last the once hotly contested battleground differs from none of its quiet surroundings, except, perhaps, that here the flowers take a richer tint and the grasses a deeper emerald.

It is thus the battle lines may be obliterated by Time, but there are left other and more lasting relics of the struggle. That dinted army sabre, with a bit of faded crape knotted at its hilt, which hangs over the mantel-piece of the "best room" of many a town and country house in these States, is one; and the graven headstone of the fallen hero is another. The old swords will be treasured and handed down from generation to generation as priceless heirlooms, and with them, let us trust, will be cherished the custom of dressing with annual flowers the resting-places of those who fell during the Civil War.

With the tears a Land hath shed
  Their graves should ever be green.

Ever their fair, true glory
  Fondly should fame rehearse —
Light of legend and story,
  Flower of marble and verse.

The impulse which led us to set apart a day for decorating the graves of our soldiers sprung from the grieved heart of the nation, and in our own time there is little chance of the rite being neglected. But the generations that come after us should not allow the observance to fall into disuse. What with us is an expression of fresh love and sorrow, should be with them an acknowledgment of an incalculable debt.

Decoration Day is the most beautiful of our national holidays. How different from those sullen batteries which used to go rumbling through our streets are the crowds of light carriages, laden with flowers and greenery, wending their way to the neighboring cemeteries! The grim cannon have turned into palm branches, and the shell and shrapnel into peach blooms. There is no hint of war in these gay baggage trains, except the presence of men in undress uniform, and perhaps here and there an empty sleeve to remind one of what has been. Year by year that empty sleeve is less in evidence.

The observance of Decoration Day is unmarked by that disorder and confusion common enough with our people in their holiday moods. The earlier sorrow has faded out of the hour, leaving a softened solemnity. It quickly ceased to be simply a local commemoration. While the sequestered country churchyards and burial-places near our great northern cities were being hung with May garlands, the thought could not but come to us that there were graves lying southward above which bent a grief as tender and sacred as our own. Invisibly we dropped unseen flowers upon those mounds. There is a beautiful significance in the fact that, two years after the close of the war, the women of Columbus, Mississippi, laid their offerings alike on Northern and Southern graves. When all is said, the great Nation has but one heart.

WRITERS AND TALKERS

As a class, literary men do not shine in conversation. The scintillating and playful essayist whom you pictured to yourself as the most genial and entertaining of companions, turns out to be a shy and untalkable individual, who chills you with his reticence when you chance to meet him. The poet whose fascinating volume you always drop into your gripsack on your summer vacation — the poet whom you have so long desired to know personally — is a moody and abstracted middle-aged gentleman, who fails to catch your name on introduction, and seems the avatar of the commonplace. The witty and ferocious critic whom your fancy had painted as a literary cannibal with a morbid appetite for tender young poets — the writer of those caustic and scholarly reviews which you never neglect to read — destroys the un-lifelike portrait you had drawn by appearing before you as a personage of slender limb and deprecating glance, who stammers and makes a painful spectacle of himself when you ask him his opinion of "The Glees of the Gulches," by Popocatepetl

Jones. The slender, dark-haired novelist of your imagination, with epigrammatic points to his mustache, suddenly takes the shape of a short, smoothly-shaven blond man, whose conversation does not sparkle at all, and you were on the lookout for the most brilliant of verbal fireworks. Perhaps it is a dramatist you have idealized. Fresh from witnessing his delightful comedy of manners, you meet him face to face only to discover that his own manners are anything but delightful. The play and the playwright are two very distinct entities. You grow skeptical touching the truth of Buffon's assertion that the style is the man himself. Who that has encountered his favorite author in the flesh has not sometimes been a little, if not wholly, disappointed?

After all, is it not expecting too much to expect a novelist to talk as cleverly as the clever characters in his novels? Must a dramatist necessarily go about armed to the teeth with crisp dialogue? May not a poet be allowed to lay aside his singing-robes and put on a conventional dress-suit when he dines out? Why is it not permissible in him to be as prosaic and tiresome as the rest of the company? He usually is.

ON EARLY RISING

A CERTAIN scientific gentleman of my acquaintance, who has devoted years to investigating the subject, states that he has never come across a case of remarkable longevity unaccompanied by the habit of early rising; from which testimony it might be inferred that they die early who lie abed late. But this would be getting out at the wrong station. That the majority of elderly persons are early risers is due to the simple fact that they cannot sleep mornings. After a man passes his fiftieth milestone he usually awakens at dawn, and his wakefulness is no credit to him. As the theorist confined his observations to the aged, he easily reached the conclusion that men live to be old because they do not sleep late, instead of perceiving that men do not sleep late because they are old. He moreover failed to take into account the numberless young lives that have been shortened by matutinal habits.

The intelligent reader, and no other is supposable, need not be told that the early bird aphorism is a warning and not an incentive.

The fate of the worm refutes the pretended ethical teaching of the proverb, which assumes to illustrate the advantage of early rising and does so by showing how extremely dangerous it is. I have no patience with the worm, and when I rise with the lark I am always careful to select a lark that has overslept himself.

The example set by this mythical bird, a mythical bird so far as New England is concerned, has wrought wide-spread mischief and discomfort. It is worth noting that his method of accomplishing these ends is directly the reverse of that of the Caribbean insect mentioned by Lafcadio Hearn, in his enchanting "Two Years in the French West Indies"— a species of colossal cricket called the wood-kid; in the creole tongue, *cabritt-bois*. This ingenious pest works a soothing, sleep-compelling chant from sundown until precisely half past four in the morning, when it suddenly stops and by its silence awakens everybody it has lulled into slumber with its insidious croon. Mr. Hearn, with strange obtuseness to the enormity of the thing, blandly remarks: "For thousands of early risers too poor to own a clock, the cessation of its song is the signal to get up." I devoutly trust that none of the West India islands furnishing such satanic entomological specimens will ever be annexed to the United States. Some of our extreme advocates of territorial expansion might spend a profitable few weeks on one of those favored isles. A brief association with that *cabritt-bois* would be likely to cool the enthusiasm of the most ardent imperialist.

An incalculable amount of specious sentiment has been lavished upon daybreak, chiefly by poets who breakfasted, when they did breakfast, at mid-day. It is charitably to be said that their practice was better than their precept — or their poetry. Thomson, the author of "The Castle of Indolence," who gave birth to the depraved apostrophe,

> Falsely luxurious, will not man awake,

was one of the laziest men of his century. He customarily lay in bed until noon meditating pentameters on sunrise. This creature used to be seen in his garden of an afternoon, with both hands in his waistcoat pockets, eating peaches from a pendent bough. Nearly all the English poets who at that epoch celebrated what they called "the effulgent orb of day" were denizens of London, where pure sunshine is unknown eleven months out of the twelve.

In a great city there are few incentives to early rising. What charm is there in roof-tops and chimney-stacks to induce one to escape even from a nightmare? What is more depressing than a city street before the shop-windows have lifted an eyelid, when "the very houses seem asleep," as Wordsworth says, and nobody is astir but the belated burglar or the milk-and-water man or Mary washing off the front steps? Daybreak at the seaside or up among the mountains is sometimes worth while, though familiarity with it breeds indifference. The man forced by restlessness or occupation to drink the first vintage of the morning every day of his life has no right appreciation of the beverage, however much he may profess to relish it. It is only your habitual late riser who takes in the full flavor of Nature at those rare intervals when he gets up to go a-fishing. He brings virginal emotions and unsatiated eyes to the sparkling freshness of earth and stream and sky. For him — a momentary Adam — the world is newly created. It is Eden come again, with Eve in the similitude of a three-pound trout.

In the country, then, it is well enough occasionally to dress by candle-light and assist at the ceremony of dawn; it is well if for no other purpose than to disarm the intolerance of the professional early riser who, were he in a state of perfect health, would not be the wandering victim of insomnia, and boast of it. There are few small things more exasperating than this early bird with the worm of his conceit in his bill.

UN POÊTE MANQUÉ

In the first volume of Miss Dickinson's poetical mélange is a little poem which needs only a slight revision of the initial stanza to entitle it to rank with some of the swallow-flights in Heine's lyrical intermezzo. I have tentatively tucked a rhyme into that opening stanza:

> I taste a liquor never brewed
> In vats upon the Rhine;
> No tankard ever held a draught
> Of alcohol like mine.
>
> Inebriate of air am I,
> And debauchee of dew,
> Reeling, through endless summer days,
> From inns of molten blue.
>
> When landlords turn the drunken bee
> Out of the Foxglove's door,
> When butterflies renounce their drams,
> I shall but drink the more!
>
> Till seraphs swing their snowy caps
> And saints to windows run,
> To see the little tippler
> Leaning against the sun!

Those inns of molten blue, and the disreputable honey-gatherer who gets himself turned out-of-doors at the sign of the Foxglove, are very taking matters. I know of more important things that interest me vastly less. This is one of the ten or twelve brief pieces so nearly perfect in structure as almost to warrant the reader in suspecting that Miss Dickinson's general disregard of form was a deliberate affectation. The artistic finish of the following sunset-piece makes her usual quatrains unforgivable:

> This is the land the sunset washes,
> These are the banks of the Yellow Sea;
> Where it rose, or whither it rushes,
> These are the western mystery!
>
> Night after night her purple traffic
> Strews the landing with opal bales;
> Merchantmen poise upon horizons,
> Dip, and vanish with fairy sails.

The little picture has all the opaline atmosphere of a Claude Lorraine. One instantly frames it in one's memory. Several such bits of impressionist landscape may be found in the portfolio.

It is to be said, in passing, that there are few things in Miss Dickinson's poetry so felicitous as Mr. Higginson's characterization of it in his preface to the volume: "In many cases these verses will seem to the reader *like poetry pulled up by the roots,* with rain and dew and earth clinging to them." Possibly it might be objected that this is not the best way to gather either flowers or poetry.

Miss Dickinson possessed an extremely unconventional and bizarre mind. She was deeply tinged by the mysticism of Blake, and strongly influenced by the mannerism of Emerson. The very gesture with which she tied her bonnet-strings, preparatory to one of her nun-like walks in her claustral garden at Amherst, must have had something dreamy and Emersonian in it. She had much fancy of a quaint kind, but only, as it appears to me, intermittent flashes of imagination.

That Miss Dickinson's memoranda have a certain something which, for want of a more precise name, we term *quality*, is not to be denied. But the incoherence and shapelessness of the greater part of her verse are fatal. On nearly every page one lights upon an unsupported exquisite line or a lonely happy epithet ; but a single happy epithet or an isolated exquisite line does not constitute a poem. What Lowell says of Dr. Donne is full of salient verses that would take the rudest March winds of criticism with their beauty, of thoughts that first tease us like charades and then delight us with the felicity of their solution ; but these have not saved him. He is exiled to the limbo of the formless and the fragmentary."

Touching this question of mere technique Mr. Ruskin has a word to say (it appears that he said it "in his earlier and better days"), and Mr. Higginson quotes it: "No weight, nor mass, nor beauty of execution can outweigh one grain or fragment of thought." This is a proposition to which one would cordially subscribe if it were not so intemperately stated. A suggestive commentary on Mr. Ruskin's impressive dictum is furnished by his own volume of verse. The substance of it is weighty enough, but the workmanship lacks just that touch which distinguishes the artist from the bungler — the touch which Mr. Ruskin, except when writing prose, appears not much to have regarded either in his later or "in his earlier and better days."

Miss Dickinson's stanzas, with their impossible rhyme, their involved significance, their interrupted flute-note of birds that have no continuous music, seem to have caught the ear of a group of eager listeners. A shy New England bluebird, shifting its light load of song, has for the moment been mistaken for a stray nightingale.

THE MALE COSTUME OF THE PERIOD

I WENT to see a play the other night, one of those good old-fashioned English comedies that are in five acts and seem to be in fifteen. The piece with its wrinkled conventionality, its archaic stiffness, and obsolete code of morals, was devoid of interest excepting as a collection of dramatic curios. Still I managed to sit it through. The one thing in it that held me a pleased spectator was the graceful costume of a certain player who looked like a fine old portrait — by Vandyke or Velasquez, let us say — that had come to life and kicked off its tarnished frame.

I do not know at what epoch of the world's history the scene of the play was laid; possibly the author originally knew, but it was evident that the actors did not, for their make-ups represented quite antagonistic periods. This circumstance, however, detracted only slightly from the special pleasure I took in the young person called Delorme. He was not in himself interesting; he was like that Major Waters in "Pepys's Diary," — "a most amorous melancholy gentleman who is under a despayr in love, which makes him bad company;" it was entirely Delorme's dress.

I never saw mortal man in a dress more sensible and becoming. The material was according to Polonius's dictum, rich but not gaudy, of some dark cherry-colored stuff with trimmings of a deeper shade. My idea of a doublet is so misty that I shall not venture to affirm that the gentleman wore a doublet. It was a loose coat of some description hanging negligently from the shoulders and looped at the throat, showing a tasteful arrangement of lacework below and at the wrists. Full trousers reaching to the tops of buckskin boots, and a low-crowned soft hat — not a Puritan's sugar-loaf, but a picturesque shapeless head-gear, one side jauntily fastened up with a jewel — completed the essential portions of our friend's attire. It was a costume to walk in, to ride in, to sit in. The wearer of it could not be awkward if he tried, and I will do Delorme the justice to say that he put his dress to some severe tests. But he was graceful all the while, and made me wish that my countrymen would throw aside their present hideous habiliments and hasten to the measuring-room of Delorme's tailor.

In looking over the plates of an old book of fashions we smile at the monstrous attire in which our worthy great-grandsires saw fit to deck themselves. Presently it will be the turn of prosperity to smile at us, for in our own way we are no less ridiculous than were our ancestors in their knee-breeches, pig-tail, and *chapeau de bras*. In fact, we are really more absurd. If a fashionably dressed man of to-day could catch a single glimpse of himself through the eyes of his descendants four or five generations removed, he would have a strong impression of being something that had escaped from somewhere.

Whatever strides we may have made in arts and sciences, we have made no advance in the matter of costume. That Americans do not tattoo themselves, and do go fully clad — I am speaking exclusively of my own sex —is about all that can be said in favor of our present fashions. I wish I had the vocabulary of Herr Teufelsdröckh with which to inveigh against the dress-coat of our evening parties, the angular swallow-tailed coat that makes a man look like a poor species of bird and gets him mistaken for the waiter. "As long as a man wears the modern coat," says Leigh Hunt, "he has no right to despise any dress. What snips at the collar and lapels! What a mechanical and ridiculous cut about the flaps! What buttons in front that are never meant to button, and yet are no ornament! And what an exquisitely absurd pair of buttons at the back! gravely regarded, nevertheless, and thought as indispensably necessary to every well-conditioned coat, as other bits of metal or bone are to the bodies of savages whom we laugh at. There is absolutely not one iota of sense, grace, or even economy in the modern coat."

Still more deplorable is the ceremonial hat of the period. That a Christian can go about unabashed with a shiny black cylinder on his head shows what civilization has done for us in the way of taste in personal decoration. The scalp-lock of an Apache brave has more style. When an Indian squaw comes into a frontier settlement, the first "marked-down" article she purchases is a section of stove-pipe. Her instinct as to the eternal fitness of things tells her that its proper place is on the skull of a barbarian.

It was while revolving these pleasing reflections in my mind that our friend Delorme walked across the stage in the fourth act, and though there was nothing in the situation nor in the text of the play to warrant it, I broke into tremendous applause, from which I desisted only at the scowl of an usher — an object in a celluloid collar and a claw-hammer coat. My solitary ovation to Master Delorme was an involuntary and, I think, pardonable protest against the male costume of our own time.

ON A CERTAIN AFFECTATION

EXCEPTING on the ground that youth is the age of vain fantasy, there is no accounting for the fact that young men and young women of poetical temperament should so frequently assume to look upon an early demise for themselves as the most desirable thing in the world. Though one may incidentally be tempted to agree with them in the abstract, one cannot help wondering. That persons who are exceptionally fortunate in their environment, and in private do not pretend to be otherwise, should openly announce their intention of retiring at once into the family tomb, is a problem not easily solved. The public has so long listened to these funereal solos that if a few of the poets thus impatient to be gone were to go, their departure would perhaps be attended by that resigned speeding which the proverb invokes on behalf of the parting guest.

The existence of at least one magazine editor would, I know, have a shadow lifted from it. At this writing, in a small mortuary basket under his desk are seven or eight poems of so gloomy a nature that he would not be able to remain in the same room with them if he did not suspect the integrity of their pessimism. The ring of a false coin is not more recognizable than that of a rhyme setting forth a simulated sorrow.

The Miss Gladys who sends a poem entitled "Forsaken," in which she addresses death as her only friend, makes pictures in the editor's eyes. He sees, among other dissolving views, a little hoyden in magnificent spirits, perhaps one of this season's social buds, with half a score of lovers ready to pluck her from the family stem — a rose whose countless petals are coupons. A caramel has disagreed with her, or she would not have written in this despondent vein. The young man who seeks to inform the world in eleven anæmic stanzas of *terze rime* that the cup of happiness has been forever dashed from his lip (he appears to have but one), and darkly intimates when the end is "nigh" (rhyming affably with "sigh"), will probably be engaged a quarter of a century from now in making similar declarations. He is simply echoing some dysthymic poet of the past — reaching out with some other man's hat for the stray nickel of your sympathy.

This morbidness seldom accompanies genuine poetic gifts. The case of David Gray, the young Scottish poet who died in 1861, is an instance to the contrary. His lot was exceedingly sad, and the failure of health just as he was on the verge of achieving something like success justified his profound melancholy; but that he tuned this melancholy and played upon it, as if it were a musical instrument, is plainly seen in one of his sonnets.

In Monckton Milnes's (Lord Houghton's) "Life and Letters of John Keats" it is related that Keats, one day, on finding a stain of blood upon his lips after coughing, said to his friend Charles Brown: "I know the color of that blood; it is arterial blood; I cannot be deceived. That drop is my death-warrant. I must die." Who that ever read the passage could forget it? David Gray did not, for he versified the incident as happening to himself, and appropriated, as his own, Keats's comment:

> Last night, on coughing slightly with sharp pain,
> There came arterial blood, and with a sigh
> Of absolute grief I cried in bitter vein,
> That drop is my death-warrant; I must die.

The incident was likely enough a personal experience, but the comment should have been placed in quotation marks. I know of few stranger things in literature than this poet's dramatization of another man's pathos. Even Keats's epitaph — *Here lies one whose name was writ in water* — finds an echo in David Gray's *Below lies one whose name was traced in sand.* Poor Gray was, at least, the better prophet.

WISHMAKERS' TOWN

A LIMITED edition of this little volume of verse, which seems to me in many respects unique, was issued in 1885, and has long been out of print. The reissue of the book is in response to the desire of certain readers who have not forgotten the charm which William Young's poem exercised upon them years ago, and, finding the charm still potent, would have others share it.

The scheme of the poem, for it is a poem and not simply a series of unrelated lyrics, is ingenious and original, and unfolds itself in measures at once strong and delicate. The mood of the poet and the method of the playwright are obvious throughout. Wishmakers' Town — a little town situated in the no-man's-land of "The Tempest" and "A Midsummer Night's Dream" — is shown to us as it awakens, touched by the dawn. The clangor of bells far and near calls the townfolk to their various avocations, the toiler to his toil, the idler to his idleness, the miser to his gold. In swift and picturesque sequence the personages of the Masque pass before us. Merchants, hucksters, players, lovers, gossips, soldiers, vagabonds, and princes crowd the scene, and have in turn their word of poignant speech. We mingle with the throng in the streets; we hear the whir of looms and the din of foundries, the blare of trumpets, the whisper of lovers, the scandals of the market-place, and, in brief, are let into all the secret of the busy microcosm. A contracted stage, indeed, yet large enough for the play of many passions, as the narrowest hearthstone may be. With the sounding of the curfew, the town is hushed to sleep again, and the curtain falls on this mimic drama of life.

The charm of it all is not easily to be defined. Perhaps if one could name it, the spell were broken. Above the changing rhythms hangs an atmosphere too evasive for measurement — an atmosphere that stipulates an imaginative mood on the part of the reader. The quality which pleases in certain of the lyrical episodes is less intangible. One readily explains one's liking for so gracious a lyric as "The Flower-Seller," to select an example at random. Next to the pleasure that lies in the writing of such exquisite verse is the pleasure of quoting it. I copy the stanzas partly for my own gratification, and partly to win the reader to "Wishmakers' Town," not knowing better how to do it.

Myrtle and eglantine,
For the old love and the new!
And the columbine,
With its cap and bells, for folly!
And the daffodil, for the hopes of youth! and the rue,
For melancholy!
But of all the blossoms that blow,
Fair gallants all, I charge you to win, if ye may,
This gentle guest,
Who dreams apart, in her wimple of purple and gray,
Like the blessed Virgin, with meek head bending low
Upon her breast.
For the orange flower
Ye may buy as ye will: but the violet of the wood
Is the love of maidenhood;
And he that hath worn it but once, though but for an hour,
He shall never again, though he wander by many a stream,
No, never again shall he meet with a flower that shall seem
So sweet and pure; and forever, in after years,
At the thought of its bloom, or the fragrance of its breath,
The past shall arise,
And his eyes shall be dim with tears,
And his soul shall be far in the gardens of Paradise
Though he stand in the shambles of death.

In a different tone, but displaying the same sureness of execution, is the cry of the lowly folk, the wretched pawns in the great game of life:

Prince, and Bishop, and Knight, and Dame,
  Plot, and plunder, and disagree!
Oh, but the game is a royal game!
  Oh, but your tourneys are fair to see!

None too hopeful we found our lives;
  Sore was labor from day to day;

Still we strove for our babes and wives —
Now, to the trumpet, we march away!

"Why?" — For some one hath will'd it so!
Nothing we know of the why, or the where —
To swamp, or jungle, or wastes of snow —
Nothing we know, and little we care.

Give us to kill! — since this is the end
Of love and labor in Nature's plan;
Give us to kill and ravish and rend,
Yea, since this is the end of man.

States shall perish and states be born:
Leaders, out of the throng, shall press;
Some to honor and some to scorn:
We, that are little, shall yet be less.

Over our lines shall the vultures soar;
Hard on our flanks shall the jackals cry;
And the dead shall be as the sands of the shore;
And daily the living shall pray to die.

Nay, what matter! — When all is said,
Prince and Bishop will plunder still:
Lord and Lady must dance and wed.
Pity us, pray for us, ye that will!

It is only the fear of impinging on Mr. Young's copyright that prevents me reprinting the graphic ballad of "The Wanderer" and the prologue of "The Strollers," which reads like a page from the prelude to some Old-World miracle play. The setting of these things is frequently antique, but the thought is the thought of to-day. I think there is a new generation of readers for such poetry as Mr. Young's. I venture the prophecy that it will not lack for them later when the time comes for the inevitable rearrangement of present poetic values.

The author of "Wishmakers' Town" is the child of his period, and has not escaped the *maladie du siècle.* The doubt and pessimism that marked the end of the nineteenth century find a voice in the bell-like strophes with which the volume closes. It is the dramatist rather than the poet who speaks here. The real message of the poet to mankind is ever one of hope. Amid the problems that perplex and discourage, it is for him to sing

> Of what the world shall be
> When the years have died away.

HISTORICAL NOVELS

In default of such an admirable piece of work as Dr. Weir Mitchell's "Hugh Wynne," I like best those fictions which deal with kingdoms and principalities that exist only in the mind's eye. One's knowledge of actual events and real personages runs no serious risk of receiving shocks in this no-man's-land. Everything that happens in an imaginary realm — in the realm of Ruritania, for illustration — has an air of possibility, at least a shadowy vraisemblance. The atmosphere and local color, having an authenticity of their own, are not to be challenged. You cannot charge the writer with ignorance of the period in which his narrative is laid, since the period is as vague as the geography. He walks on safe ground, eluding many of the perils that beset the story-teller who ventures to stray beyond the bounds of the make-believe. One peril he cannot escape, — that of misrepresenting human nature.

The anachronisms of the average historical novel, pretending to reflect history, are among its minor defects. It is a thing altogether wonderfully and fearfully made — the imbecile intrigue, the cast-iron characters, the plumed and armored dialogue with its lance of gory rhetoric forever at charge. The stage at its worst moments is not so unreal. Here art has broken into smithereens the mirror which she is supposed to hold up to nature.

In this romance world somebody is always somebody's unsuspected father, mother, or child, deceiving every one excepting the reader. Usually the anonymous person is the hero, to whom it is mere recreation to hold twenty swordsmen at bay on a staircase, killing ten or twelve of them before he escapes through a door that ever providentially opens directly behind him. How tired one gets of that door! The "caitiff" in these chronicles of when knighthood was in flower is invariably hanged from "the highest battlement" — the second highest would not do at all; or else he is thrown into "the deepest dungeon of the castle" — the second deepest dungeon was never known to be used on these occasions. The hero habitually "cleaves" his foeman "to the midriff," the "midriff" being what the properly brought up hero always has in view. A certain fictional historian of my acquaintance makes his swashbuckler exclaim: "My sword will [shall] kiss his midriff;" but that is an exceptionally lofty flight of diction.

My friend's heroine dresses as a page, and in the course of long interviews with her lover remains unrecognized — a diaphanous literary invention that must have been old when the Pyramids were young. The heroine's small brother, with playful archaicism called "a springald," puts on her skirts and things and passes himself off for his sister or anybody else he pleases. In brief, there is no puerility that is not at home in this sphere of misbegotten effort. Listen — a priest, a princess, and a young man in woman's clothes are on the scene:

> The Princess rose to her feet and approached the priest.
>
> "Father," she said swiftly, "this is not the Lady Joan, my brother's wife, but a youth marvelously like her, who hath offered himself in her place that she might escape. . . . He is the Count von Löen, a lord of Kemsburg. And I love him. We want you to marry us now, dear Father — now, without a moment's delay; for if you do not they will kill him, and I shall have to marry Prince Wasp!"

This is from "Joan of the Sword Hand," and if ever I read a more silly performance I have forgotten it.

POOR YORICK

THERE is extant in the city of New York an odd piece of bric-à-brac which I am sometimes tempted to wish was in my own possession. On a bracket in Edwin Booth's bedroom at The Players — the apartment remains as he left it that solemn June day ten years ago — stands a sadly dilapidated skull which the elder Booth, and afterward his son Edwin, used to soliloquize over in the graveyard at Elsinore in the fifth act of "Hamlet."

A skull is an object that always invokes interest more or less poignant; it always has its pathetic story, whether told or untold; but this skull is especially a skull "with a past."

In the early forties, while playing an engagement somewhere in the wild West, Junius Brutus Booth did a series of kindnesses to a particularly undeserving fellow, the name of him unknown to us. The man, as it seemed, was a combination of gambler, horse-stealer, and highwayman — in brief, a miscellaneous desperado, and precisely the melodramatic sort of person likely to touch the sympathies of the half-mad player. In the course of nature or the law, presumably the law, the adventurer bodily disappeared one day, and soon ceased to exist even as a reminiscence in the florid mind of his sometime benefactor.

As the elder Booth was seated at breakfast one morning in a hotel in Louisville, Kentucky, a negro boy entered the room bearing a small osier basket neatly covered with a snowy napkin. It had the general appearance of a basket of fruit or flowers sent by some admirer, and as such it figured for a moment in Mr. Booth's conjecture. On lifting the cloth the actor started from the chair with a genuine expression on his features of that terror which he was used so marvelously to simulate as Richard III in the midnight tent-scene or as Macbeth when the ghost of Banquo usurped his seat at table.

In the pretty willow-woven basket lay the head of Booth's old pensioner, which head the old pensioner had bequeathed in due legal form to the tragedian, begging him henceforth to adopt it as one of the necessary stage properties in the fifth act of Mr. Shakespeare's tragedy of "Hamlet." "Take it away, you black imp!" thundered the actor, to the equally aghast negro boy, whose curiosity had happily not prompted him to investigate the dark nature of his burden.

Shortly afterward, however, the horse-stealer's

residuary legatee, recovering from the first shock of his surprise, fell into the grim humor of the situation, and proceeded to carry out to the letter the testator's whimsical request. Thus it was that the skull came to secure an engagement to play the rôle of poor Yorick in J. B. Booth's company of strolling players, and to continue awhile longer to glimmer behind the footlights in the hands of his famous son.

Observing that the grave-digger in his too eager realism was damaging the thing, — the marks of his pick and spade are visible on the cranium, — Edwin Booth presently replaced it with a papier-maché counterfeit manufactured in the property room of the theatre. During his subsequent wanderings in Australia and California, he carefully preserved the relic, which finally found repose on the bracket in question.

How often have I sat, of an afternoon, in that front room on the fourth floor of the club-house in Gramercy Park, watching the winter or summer twilight gradually softening and blurring the sharp outline of the skull until it vanished uncannily into the gloom! Edwin Booth had forgotten, if ever he knew, the name of the man; but I had no need of it in order to establish acquaintance with poor Yorick. In this association I was conscious of a deep tinge of sentiment on my own part, a circumstance not without its queerness, considering how very distant the acquaintance really was.

Possibly he was a fellow of infinite jest in his day ; he was sober enough now, and in no way disposed to indulge in those flashes of merriment "that were wont to set the table on a roar." But I did not regret his evaporated hilarity; I liked his more befitting genial silence, and had learned to look upon his rather open countenance with the same friendliness as that with which I regarded the faces of less phantasmal members of the club. He had become to me a dramatic personality as distinct as that of any of the Thespians I met in the grill-room or the library.

Yorick's feeling in regard to me was a subject upon which I frequently speculated. There was at intervals an alert gleam of intelligence in those cavernous eye-sockets, as if the sudden remembrance of some old experience had illumined them. He had been a great traveler, and had known strange vicissitudes in life; his stage career had brought him into contact with a varied assortment of men and women, and extended his horizon. His more peaceful profession of holding up mail-coaches on lonely roads had surely not been without incident. It was inconceivable that all this had left no impressions. He must have had at least a faint recollection of the tempestuous Junius Brutus Booth. That Yorick had formed his estimate of me, and probably not a flattering one, is something of which I am strongly convinced.

At the death of Edwin Booth, poor Yorick passed out of my personal cognizance, and now lingers an incongruous shadow amid the memories of the precious things I lost then.

The suite of apartments formerly occupied by Edwin Booth at The Players has been, as I have said, kept unchanged—a shrine to which from time to time some loving heart makes silent pilgrimage. On a table in the centre of his bedroom lies the book just where he laid it down, an ivory paper-cutter marking the page his eyes last rested upon; and in this chamber, with its familiar pictures, pipes, and ornaments, the skull finds its proper sanctuary. If at odd moments I wish that by chance poor Yorick had fallen to my care, the wish is only half-hearted; though had that happened, I would have given him welcome to the choicest corner in my study and tenderly cherished him for the sake of one who comes no more.

THE AUTOGRAPH HUNTER

One that gathers samphire, dreadful trade! — *King Lear.*

THE material for this paper on the autograph hunter, his ways and his manners, has been drawn chiefly from experiences not my own. My personal relations with him have been comparatively restricted, a circumstance to which I owe the privilege of treating the subject with a freedom that might otherwise not seem becoming.

No author is insensible to the compliment involved in a request for his autograph, assuming the request to come from some sincere lover of books and bookmen. It is an affair of different complexion when he is importuned to give time and attention to the innumerable unknown who "collect" autographs as they would collect postage stamps, with no interest in the matter beyond the desire to accumulate as many as possible. The average autograph hunter, with his purposeless insistence, reminds one of the queen in Stockton's story whose fad was "the buttonholes of all nations."

In our population of eighty millions and upwards there are probably two hundred thousand persons interested more or less in what is termed the literary world. This estimate is absurdly low, but it serves to cast a sufficient side-light upon the situation. Now, any unit of these two hundred thousand is likely at any moment to indite a letter to some favorite novelist, historian, poet, or what not. It will be seen, then, that the autograph hunter is no inconsiderable person. He has made it embarrassing work for the author fortunate or unfortunate enough to be regarded as worth while. Every mail adds to his reproachful pile of unanswered letters. If he have a conscience, and no amanuensis, he quickly finds himself tangled in the meshes of endless and futile correspondence. Through policy, good nature, or vanity he is apt to become facile prey.

A certain literary collector once confessed in print that he always studied the idiosyncrasies of his "subject" as carefully as another sort of collector studies the plan of the house to which he meditates a midnight visit. We were assured that with skillful preparation and adroit approach an autograph could be extracted from anybody. According to the revelations of the writer, Bismarck, Queen Victoria, and Mr. Gladstone had their respective point of easy access, —their one unfastened door or window, metaphorically speaking. The strongest man has his weak side.

Dr. Holmes's affability in replying to every one who wrote to him was perhaps not a trait characteristic of the elder group. Mr. Lowell, for instance, was harder-hearted and rather difficult to reach. I recall one day in the library at Elmwood. As I was taking down a volume from the shelf a sealed letter escaped from the pages and fluttered to my feet. I handed it to Mr. Lowell, who glanced incuriously at the superscription. "Oh, yes," he said, smiling, "I know 'em by instinct." Relieved of its envelope, the missive turned out to be eighteen months old, and began with the usual amusing solecism: "As one of the most famous of American authors I would like to possess your autograph."

Each recipient of such requests has of course his own way of responding. Mr. Whittier used to be obliging; Mr. Longfellow politic; Mr. Emerson, always philosophical, dreamily confiscated the postage stamps.

Time was when the collector contented himself with a signature on a card; but that, I am told, no longer satisfies. He must have a letter addressed to him personally—"on any subject you please," as an immature scribe lately suggested to an acquaintance of mine. The ingenuous youth purposed to flourish a letter in the faces of his less fortunate competitors, in order to show them that he was on familiar terms with the celebrated So-and-So. This or a kindred motive is a spur to many a collector. The stratagems he employs to compass his end are inexhaustible. He drops you an off-hand note to inquire in what year you first published your beautiful poem entitled "A Psalm of Life." If you are a simple soul, you hasten to assure him that you are not the author of that poem, which he must have confused with your "Rime of the Ancient Mariner"—and there you are. Another expedient is to ask if your father's middle name was not Hierophilus. Now, your father has probably been dead many years, and as perhaps he was not a public man in his day, you are naturally touched that any one should have interest in him after this long flight of time. In the innocence of your heart you reply by the next mail that your father's middle name was not Hierophilus, but Epaminondas—and there you are again. It is humiliating to be caught swinging, like a simian ancestor, on a branch of one's genealogical tree.

Some morning you find beside your plate at breakfast an imposing parchment with a great gold seal in the upper left-hand corner. This document—I am relating an actual occurrence—announces with a flourish that you have unanimously been elected an honorary member of

The Kalamazoo International Literary Association. Possibly the honor does not take away your respiration; but you are bound by courtesy to make an acknowledgment, and you express your insincere thanks to the obliging secretary of a literary organization which does not exist anywhere on earth.

A scheme of lighter creative touch is that of the correspondent who advises you that he is replenishing his library and desires a detailed list of your works, with the respective dates of their first issue, price, style of binding, etc. A bibliophile, you say to yourself. These interrogations should of course have been addressed to your publisher; but they are addressed to you, with the stereotyped "thanks in advance." The natural inference is that the correspondent, who writes in a brisk commercial vein, wishes to fill out his collection of your books, or, possibly, to treat himself to a complete set in full crushed Levant. Eight or ten months later this individual, having forgotten (or hoping you will not remember) that he has already demanded a chronological list of your writings, forwards another application couched in the self-same words. The length of time it takes him to "replenish" his library (with your books) strikes you as pathetic. You cannot control your emotions sufficiently to pen a reply. From a purely literary point of view this gentleman cares nothing whatever for your holograph; from a mercantile point of view he cares greatly and likes to obtain duplicate specimens, which he disposes of to dealers in such frail merchandise.

The pseudo-journalist who is engaged in preparing a critical and biographical sketch of you, and wants to incorporate, if possible, some slight hitherto unnoted event in your life — a signed photograph and a copy of your book-plate are here in order — is also a character which periodically appears upon the scene. In this little Comedy of Deceptions there are as many players as men have fancies.

A brother slave-of-the-lamp permits me to transfer this leaf from the book of his experience: "Not long ago the postman brought me a letter of a rather touching kind. The unknown writer, lately a widow, and plainly a woman of refinement, had just suffered a new affliction in the loss of her little girl. My correspondent asked me to copy for her ten or a dozen lines from a poem which I had written years before on the death of a child. The request was so shrinkingly put, with such an appealing air of doubt as to its being heeded, that I immediately transcribed the entire poem, a matter of a hundred lines or so, and sent it to her. I am unable to this day to decide whether I was wholly hurt or wholly amused when, two months afterward, I stumbled over my manuscript, with a neat price attached to it, in a second-hand bookshop."

Perhaps the most distressing feature of the whole business is the very poor health which seems to prevail among autograph hunters. No other class of persons in the community shows so large a percentage of confirmed invalids. There certainly is some mysterious connection between incipient spinal trouble and the collecting of autographs. Which superinduces the other is a question for pathology. It is a fact that one out of every eight applicants for a specimen of penmanship bases his or her claim upon the possession of some vertebral disability which leaves him or her incapable of doing anything but write to authors for their autograph. Why this particular diversion should be the sole resource remains undisclosed. But so it appears to be, and the appeal to one's sympathy is most direct and persuasive. Personally, however, I have my suspicions, suspicions that are shared by several men of letters, who have come to regard this plea of invalidism, in the majority of cases, as simply the variation of a very old and familiar tune. I firmly believe that the health of autograph hunters, as a class, is excellent.

ROBERT HERRICK

ROBERT HERRICK

I

A LITTLE over three hundred years ago England had given to her a poet of the very rarest lyrical quality, but she did not discover the fact for more than a hundred and fifty years afterward. The poet himself was aware of the fact at once, and stated it, perhaps not too modestly, in countless quatrains and couplets, which were not read, or, if read, were not much regarded at the moment. It has always been an incredulous world in this matter. So many poets have announced their arrival and not arrived!

Robert Herrick was descended in a direct line from an ancient family in Lincolnshire, the Eyricks, a mentionable representative of which was John Eyrick of Leicester, the poet's grandfather, admitted freeman in 1535, and afterward twice made mayor of the town. John Eyrick or Heyricke—he spelled his name recklessly—had five sons, the second of whom sought a career in London, where he became a goldsmith, and in December, 1582, married Julian Stone, spinster, of Bedfordshire, a sister to

Anne, Lady Soame, the wife of Sir Stephen Soame. One of the many children of this marriage was Robert Herrick.

It is the common misfortune of the poet's biographers, though it was the poet's own great good fortune, that the personal interviewer was an unknown quantity at the period when Herrick played his part on the stage of life. Of that performance, in its intimate aspects, we have only the slightest record.

Robert Herrick was born in Wood Street, Cheapside, London, in 1591, and baptized at St. Vedast's, Foster Lane, on August 24 of that year. He had several brothers and sisters, with whom we shall not concern ourselves. It would be idle to add the little we know about these persons to the little we know about Herrick himself. He is a sufficient problem without dragging in the rest of the family.

When the future lyrist was fifteen months old his father, Nicholas Herrick, made his will, and immediately fell out of an upper window. Whether or not this fall was an intended sequence to the will, the high almoner, Dr. Fletcher, Bishop of Bristol, promptly put in his claim to the estate, "all goods and chattels of suicides" becoming his by law. The circumstances were suspicious, though not conclusive, and the good bishop, after long litigation, consented to refer the case to arbitrators, who awarded him two hundred and twenty pounds, thus leaving the question at issue — whether or not Herrick's death had been his own premeditated act — still wrapped in its original mystery. This singular law, which had the possible effect of inducing high almoners to encourage suicide among well-to-do persons of the lower and middle classes, was afterwards rescinded.

Nicholas Herrick did not leave his household destitute, for his estate amounted to five thousand pounds, that is to say, twenty-five thousand pounds in to-day's money; but there were many mouths to feed. The poet's two uncles, Robert Herrick and William Herrick of Beaumanor, the latter subsequently knighted[1] for his usefulness as jeweler and money-lender to James I, were appointed guardians to the children.

Young Robert appears to have attended school in Westminster until his fifteenth year, when he was apprenticed to Sir William, who had

[1] Dr. Grosart, in his interesting and valuable Memorial-Introduction to Herrick's poems, quotes this curious item from Winwood's *Memorials of Affairs of State:* "On Easter Tuesday [1605], one Mr. William Herrick, a goldsmith in Cheapside, was Knighted for making a Hole in the great Diamond the King doth wear. The party little expected the honour, but he did his work so well as won the King to an extraordinary liking of it."

learned the gentle art of goldsmith from his nephew's father. Though Robert's indentures bound him for ten years, Sir William is supposed to have offered no remonstrance when he was asked, long before that term expired, to cancel the engagement and allow Robert to enter Cambridge, which he did as fellow-commoner at St. John's College. At the end of two years he transferred himself to Trinity Hall, with a view to economy and the pursuit of the law — the two frequently go together. He received his degree of B. A. in 1617, and his M. A. in 1620, having relinquished the law for the arts.

During this time he was assumed to be in receipt of a quarterly allowance of ten pounds — a not illiberal provision, the pound being then five times its present value; but as the payments were eccentric, the master of arts was in recurrent distress. If this money came from his own share of his father's estate, as seems likely, Herrick had cause for complaint; if otherwise, the pith is taken out of his grievance.

The Iliad of his financial woes at this juncture is told in a few chance-preserved letters written to his "most careful uncle," as he calls that evidently thrifty person. In one of these monotonous and dreary epistles, which are signed "R. Hearick," the writer says: "The essence of my writing is (as heretofore) to entreat you to paye for my use to Mr. Arthour Johnson, bookseller, in Paule's Churchyarde, the ordinarie sume of tenn pounds, and that with as much sceleritie as you maye." He also indulges in the natural wish that his college bills "had leaden wings and tortice feet." This was in 1617. The young man's patrimony, whatever it may have been, had dwindled, and he confesses to "many a throe and pinches of the purse." For the moment, at least, his prospects were not flattering.

Robert Herrick's means of livelihood, when in 1620 he quitted the university and went up to London, are conjectural. It is clear that he was not without some resources, since he did not starve to death on his wits before he discovered a patron in the Earl of Pembroke. In the court circle Herrick also unearthed humbler, but perhaps not less useful, allies in the persons of Edward Norgate, clerk of the signet, and Master John Crofts, cup-bearer to the king. Through the two New Year anthems, honored by the music of Henry Lawes, his Majesty's organist at Westminster, it is more than possible that Herrick was brought to the personal notice of Charles and Henrietta Maria. All this was a promise of success, but not success itself. It has been thought probable that Herrick may have secured some minor office in the chapel at Whitehall. That would accord with his subsequent appointment (September, 1627) as chaplain to the Duke of Buckingham's unfortunate expedition to the Isle of Rhé.

Precisely when Herrick was invested with holy orders is not ascertainable. If one may draw an inference from his poems, the life he led meanwhile was not such as his "most careful uncle" would have warmly approved. The literary clubs and coffee-houses of the day were open to a free-lance like young Herrick, some of whose blithe measures, passing in manuscript from hand to hand, had brought him faintly to light as a poet. The Dog and the Triple Tun were not places devoted to worship, unless it were to the worship of "rare Ben Jonson," at whose feet Herrick now sat, with the other blossoming young poets of the season. He was a faithful disciple to the end, and addressed many loving lyrics to the master, of which not the least graceful is "His Prayer to Ben Jonson:"

When I a verse shall make,
Know I have praid thee
For old religion's sake,
Saint Ben, to aide me.

Make the way smooth for me,
When I, thy Herrick,
Honouring thee, on my knee
Offer my lyric.

Candles I 'll give to thee,
And a new altar;
And thou, Saint Ben, shalt be
Writ in my Psalter.

On September 30, 1629, Charles I, at the recommending of the Earl of Exeter, presented Herrick with the vicarage of Dean Prior, near Totnes, in Devonshire. Here he was destined to pass the next nineteen years of his life among surroundings not congenial. For Herrick to be a mile away from London stone was for Herrick to be in exile. Even with railway and telegraphic interruptions from the outside world, the dullness of a provincial English town of to-day is something formidable. The dullness of a sequestered English hamlet in the early part of the seventeenth century must have been appalling. One is dimly conscious of a belated throb of sympathy for Robert Herrick. Yet, however discontented or unhappy he may have been at first in that lonely vicarage, the world may congratulate itself on the circumstances that stranded him there, far from the distractions of the town, and with no other solace than his Muse, for there it was he wrote the greater number of the poems which were to make his fame. It is to this accidental banishment to Devon that we owe the cluster of exquisite pieces descriptive of obsolete rural manners and customs — the Christmas masks, the Twelfth-night mummeries, the morris-dances, and the May-day festivals.

The November following Herrick's appointment to the benefice was marked by the death of his mother, who left him no heavier legacy than "a ringe of twenty shillings." Perhaps this was an understood arrangement between them; but it is to be observed that, though Herrick was a spendthrift in epitaphs, he wasted no funeral lines on Julian Herrick. In the matter of verse he dealt generously with his family down to the latest nephew. One of his most charming and touching poems is entitled "To His Dying Brother, Master William Herrick," a posthumous son. There appear to have been two brothers named William. The younger, who died early, is supposed to be referred to here.

The story of Herrick's existence at Dean Prior is as vague and bare of detail as the rest of the narrative. His parochial duties must have been irksome to him, and it is to be imagined that he wore his cassock lightly. As a preparation for ecclesiastical life he forswore sack and poetry; but presently he was with the Muse again, and his farewell to sack was in a strictly Pickwickian sense. Herrick had probably accepted the vicarship as he would have accepted a lieutenancy in a troop of horse — with an eye to present emolument and future promotion. The promotion never came, and the emolument was nearly as scant as that of Goldsmith's parson, who considered himself "passing rich with forty pounds a year" — a height of optimism beyond the reach of Herrick, with his expensive town wants and habits. But fifty pounds — the salary of his benefice — and possible perquisites in the way of marriage and burial fees would enable him to live for the time being. It was better than a possible nothing a year in London.

Herrick's religious convictions were assuredly not deeper than those of the average layman. Various writers have taken a different view of the subject; but it is inconceivable that a clergyman with a fitting sense of his function could have written certain of the poems which Herrick afterwards gave to the world — those astonishing epigrams upon his rustic enemies, and those habitual bridal compliments which, among his personal friends, must have added a terror to matrimony. Had he written only in that vein, the posterity which he so often invoked with pathetic confidence would not have greatly troubled itself about him.

It cannot positively be asserted that all the verses in question relate to the period of his incumbency, for none of his verse is dated, with the exception of the Dialogue betwixt Horace and Lydia. The date of some of the compositions may be arrived at by induction. The religious pieces grouped under the title of "Noble Numbers" distinctly associate themselves with Dean Prior, and have little other interest. Very few of them are "born of the royal blood." They lack the inspiration and magic of his secular poetry, and are frequently so fantastical and grotesque as to stir a suspicion touching the absolute soundness of Herrick's mind at all times. The lines in which the Supreme Being is assured that he may read Herrick's poems without taking any tincture from their sinfulness might have been written in a retreat for the unbalanced. "For unconscious impiety," remarks Mr. Edmund Gosse,[1] "this rivals the famous passage in which Robert Montgomery exhorted God to 'pause and think.'" Elsewhere, in an apostrophe to "Heaven," Herrick says:

> Let mercy be
> So kind to set me free,
> And I will straight
> Come in, or force the gate.

In any event, the poet did not purpose to be left out!

Relative to the inclusion of unworthy pieces and the general absence of arrangement in the

[1] In *Seventeenth-Century Studies.*

"Hesperides," Dr. Grosart advances the theory that the printers exercised arbitrary authority on these points. Dr. Grosart assumes that Herrick kept the epigrams and personal tributes in manuscript books separate from the rest of the work, which would have made a too slender volume by itself, and on the plea of this slenderness was induced to trust the two collections to the publisher, "whereupon he or some unskilled subordinate proceeded to intermix these additions with the others. That the poet himself had nothing to do with the arrangement or disarrangement lies on the surface." This is an amiable supposition, but merely a supposition. Herrick personally placed the "copy" in the hands of John Williams and Francis Eglesfield, and if he were over-persuaded to allow them to print unfit verses, and to observe no method whatever in the contents of the book, the discredit is none the less his. It is charitable to believe that Herrick's coarseness was not the coarseness of the man, but of the time, and that he followed the fashion *malgré lui*. With regard to the fairy poems, they certainly should have been given in sequence; but if there are careless printers, there are also authors who are careless in the arrangement of their manuscript, a kind of task, moreover, in which Herrick was wholly unpracticed, and might easily have made mistakes. The "Hesperides" was his sole publication.

Herrick was now thirty-eight years of age. Of his personal appearance at this time we have no description. The portrait of him prefixed to the original edition of his works belongs to a much later moment. Whether or not the bovine features in Marshall's engraving are a libel on the poet, it is to be regretted that oblivion has not laid its erasing finger on that singularly unpleasant counterfeit presentment. It is interesting to note that this same Marshall engraved the head of Milton for the first collection of his miscellaneous poems — the precious 1645 volume, containing "Il Penseroso," "Lycidas," "Comus," etc. The plate gave great offense to the serious-minded young Milton, not only because it represented him as an elderly person, but because of certain minute figures of peasant lads and lassies who are very indistinctly seen dancing frivolously under the trees in the background. Herrick had more reason to protest. The aggressive face bestowed upon him by the artist lends a tone of veracity to the tradition that the vicar occasionally hurled the manuscript of his sermon at the heads of his drowsy parishioners, accompanying the missive with pregnant remarks. He has the aspect of one meditating assault and battery.

To offset the picture there is much indirect testimony to the amiability of the man, aside from the evidence furnished by his own writings. He exhibits a fine trait in the poem on the Bishop of Lincoln's imprisonment—a poem full of deference and tenderness for a person who had evidently injured the writer, probably by opposing him in some affair of church preferment. Anthony Wood says that Herrick "became much beloved by the gentry in these parts for his florid and witty (wise) discourses." It appears that he was fond of animals, and had a pet spaniel called Tracy, which did not get away without a couplet attached to him:

> Now thou art dead, no eye shall ever see
> For shape and service spaniell like to thee.

Among the exile's chance acquaintances was a sparrow, whose elegy he also sings, comparing the bird to Lesbia's sparrow, much to the latter's disadvantage. All of Herrick's geese were swans. On the authority of Dorothy King, the daughter of a woman who served Herrick's successor at Dean Prior in 1674, we are told that the poet kept a pig, which he had taught to drink out of a tankard—a kind of instruction he was admirably qualified to impart. Dorothy was in her ninety-ninth year when she communicated this fact to Mr. Barron Field, the author of the paper on Herrick published in the "Quarterly Review" for August, 1810, and in the Boston edition[1] of the "Hesperides" attributed to Southey.

What else do we know of the vicar? A very favorite theme with Herrick was Herrick. Scattered through his book are no fewer than twenty-five pieces entitled "On Himself," not to mention numberless autobiographical hints under other captions. They are merely hints, throwing casual side-lights on his likes and dislikes, and illuminating his vanity. A whimsical personage without any very definite outlines might be evolved from these fragments. I picture him as a sort of Samuel Pepys, with perhaps less quaintness, and the poetical temperament added. Like the prince of gossips, too, he somehow gets at your affections. In one place Herrick laments the threatened failure of his eyesight (quite in what would have been Pepys's manner had Pepys written verse), and in another place he tells us of the loss of a finger. The quatrain treating of this latter

[1] The Biographical Notice prefacing this volume of The British Poets is a remarkable production, grammatically and chronologically. On page 7 the writer speaks of Herrick as living "in habits of intimacy" with Ben Jonson in 1648. If that was the case, Herrick must have taken up his quarters in Westminster Abbey, for Jonson had been dead eleven years.

catastrophe is as fantastic as some of Dr. Donne's *concetti:*

> One of the five straight branches of my hand
> Is lopt already, and the rest but stand
> Expecting when to fall, which soon will be:
> First dies the leafe, the bough next, next the tree.

With all his great show of candor Herrick really reveals as little of himself as ever poet did. One thing, however, is manifest — he understood and loved music. None but a lover could have said:

> The mellow touch of musick most doth wound
> The soule when it doth rather sigh than sound.

Or this to Julia:

> So smooth, so sweet, so silvery is thy voice,
> As could they hear, the damn'd would make no noise,
> But listen to thee walking in thy chamber
> Melting melodious words to lutes of amber.

> . . . Then let me lye
> Entranc'd, and lost confusedly;
> And by thy musick stricken mute,
> Die, and be turn'd into a lute.

Herrick never married. His modest Devonshire establishment was managed by a maidservant named Prudence Baldwin. "Fate likes fine names," says Lowell. That of Herrick's maid-of-all-work was certainly a happy meeting of gentle vowels and consonants, and has had the good fortune to be embalmed in the amber of what may be called a joyous little threnody:

In this little urne is laid
Prewdence Baldwin, once my maid;
From whose happy spark here let
Spring the purple violet.

Herrick addressed a number of poems to her before her death, which seems to have deeply touched him in his loneliness. We shall not allow a pleasing illusion to be disturbed by the flippancy of an old writer who says that "Prue was but indifferently qualified to be a tenth muse." She was a faithful handmaid, and had the merit of causing Herrick in this octave to strike a note of sincerity not usual with him:

These summer-birds did with thy master stay
The times of warmth, but then they flew away,
Leaving their poet, being now grown old,
Expos'd to all the coming winter's cold.
But thou, kind Prew, didst with my fates abide
As well the winter's as the summer's tide:
For which thy love, live with thy master here
Not two, but all the seasons of the year.

Thus much have I done for thy memory, Mistress Prew!

In spite of Herrick's disparagement of Deanbourn, which he calls "a rude river," and his characterization of Devon folk as "a people currish, churlish as the seas," the fullest and pleasantest days of his life were probably spent at Dean Prior. He was not unmindful meanwhile of the gathering political storm that was to shake England to its foundations. How anxiously, in his solitude, he watched the course of events, is attested by many of his poems. This solitude was not without its compensation. "I confess," he says,

> I ne'er invented such
> Ennobled numbers for the presse
> Than where I loath'd so much.

A man is never wholly unhappy when he is writing verses. Herrick was firmly convinced that each new lyric was a stone added to the pillar of his fame, and perhaps his sense of relief was tinged with indefinable regret when he found himself suddenly deprived of his benefice. The integrity of some of his royalistic poems is doubtful; but he was not given the benefit of the doubt by the Long Parliament, which ejected the panegyrist of young Prince Charles from the vicarage of Dean Prior, and installed in his place the venerable John Syms, a gentleman with pronounced Cromwellian views.

Herrick metaphorically snapped his fingers at the Puritans, discarded his clerical habiliments, and hastened to London to pick up such as were left of the gay-colored threads of his old experience there. Once more he would drink sack at the Triple Tun, once more he would breathe the air breathed by such poets and wits as Cotton, Denham, Shirley, Selden, and the rest. "Yes, by Saint Anne! and ginger shall be hot i' the mouth too." In the gladness of getting back "from the dull confines of the drooping west," he writes a glowing apostrophe to London — that "stony stepmother to poets." He claims to be a free-born Roman, and is proud to find himself a citizen again. According to his earlier biographers, Herrick had much ado not to starve in that same longed-for London, and fell into great misery; but Dr. Grosart disputes this, arguing, with justness, that Herrick's family, which was wealthy and influential, would not have allowed him to come to abject want. With his royalistic tendencies he may not have breathed quite freely in the atmosphere of the Commonwealth, and no doubt many tribulations fell to his lot, but among them was not poverty.

The poet was now engaged in preparing his works for the press, and a few weeks following his return to London they were issued in a single volume with the title "Hesperides; or, The Works both Humane and Divine of Robert Herrick, Esq."

The time was not ready for him. A new era had dawned — the era of the commonplace. The interval was come when Shakespeare himself was to lie in a kind of twilight. Herrick was in spirit an Elizabethan, and had strayed by chance into an artificial and prosaic age — a sylvan singing creature alighting on an alien planet. "He was too natural," says Mr. Palgrave in his "Chrysomela," "too purely poetical; he had not the learned polish, the political allusion, the tone of the city, the didactic turn, which were then and onward demanded from poetry." Yet it is strange that a public which had a relish for Edmund Waller should neglect a poet who was fifty times finer than Waller in his own specialty. What poet, then, or in the half-century that followed the Restoration, could have written "Corinna's Going a-Maying," or approached in kind the ineffable grace and perfection to be found in a score of Herrick's lyrics?

The "Hesperides" was received with chilling indifference. None of Herrick's great contemporaries has left a consecrating word concerning it. The book was not reprinted during the author's lifetime, and for more than a century after his death Herrick was virtually unread. In 1796 the "Gentleman's Magazine" copied a few of the poems, and two years later Dr. Nathan Drake published in his "Literary Hours" three critical papers on the poet, with specimens of his writings. Dr. Johnson omitted him from the "Lives of the Poets," though space was found for half a score of poetasters whose names are to be found nowhere else. In 1810 Dr. Nott, a physician of Bristol, issued a small volume of selections. It was not until 1823 that Herrick was reprinted in full. It remained for the taste of our own day to multiply editions of him.

In order to set the seal to Herrick's fame, it is now only needful that some wiseacre should attribute the authorship of the poems to some man who could not possibly have written a line of them. The opportunity presents attractions that ought to be irresistible. Excepting a handful of Herrick's college letters there is no scrap of his manuscript extant; the men who drank and jested with the poet at the Dog or the Triple Tun make no reference to him;[1] and in the wide parenthesis formed by his birth and death we find as little tangible incident as is discoverable in the briefer span of Shakespeare's fifty-two years. Here is material for profundity and ciphers!

Herrick's second sojourn in London covered the period between 1648 and 1662, during which interim he fades from sight, excepting for the instant when he is publishing his book. If he engaged in further literary work there are no evidences of it beyond one contribution to the "Lacrymæ Musarum" in 1649.

[1] With the single exception of the writer of some verses in the *Musarum Deliciæ* (1656) who mentions

> That old sack
> Young Herrick took to entertain
> The Muses in a sprightly vein.

He seems to have had lodgings, for a while at least, in St. Anne's, Westminster. With the court in exile and the grim Roundheads seated in the seats of the mighty, it was no longer the merry London of his early manhood. Time and war had thinned the ranks of friends; in the old haunts the old familiar faces were wanting. Ben Jonson was dead, Waller banished, and many another comrade "in disgrace with fortune and men's eyes." As Herrick walked through crowded Cheapside or along the dingy river-bank in those years, his thought must have turned more than once to the little vicarage in Devonshire, and lingered tenderly.

On the accession of Charles II a favorable change of wind wafted Herrick back to his former moorings at Dean Prior, the obnoxious Syms having been turned adrift. This occurred on August 24, 1662, the seventy-first anniversary of the poet's baptism. Of Herrick's movements after that, tradition does not furnish even the shadow of an outline. The only notable event concerning him is recorded twelve years later in the parish register: "Robert Herrick, vicker, was buried ye 15'' day October, 1674." He was eighty-three years old. The location of his grave is unknown. In 1857 a monument to his memory was erected in Dean Church. And this is all.

II

The details that have come down to us touching Herrick's private life are as meagre as if he had been a Marlowe or a Shakespeare. But were they as ample as could be desired they would still be unimportant compared with the single fact that in 1648 he gave to the world his "Hesperides." The environments of the man were accidental and transitory. The significant part of him we have, and that is enduring so long as wit, fancy, and melodious numbers hold a charm for mankind.

A fine thing incomparably said instantly becomes familiar, and has henceforth a sort of dateless excellence. Though it may have been said three hundred years ago, it is as modern as yesterday; though it may have been said yesterday, it has the trick of seeming to have been always in our keeping. This quality of remoteness and nearness belongs, in a striking degree, to Herrick's poems. They are as novel to-day as they were on the lips of a choice few of his contemporaries, who, in reading them in their freshness, must surely have been aware here and there of the ageless grace of old idyllic poets dead and gone.

Herrick was the bearer of no heavy message to the world, and such message as he had he was apparently in no hurry to deliver. On this point he somewhere says:

> Let others to the printing presse run fast;
> Since after death comes glory, I 'll not haste.

He had need of his patience, for he was long detained on the road by many of those obstacles that waylay poets on their journeys to the printer.

Herrick was nearly sixty years old when he published the "Hesperides." It was, I repeat, no heavy message, and the bearer was left an unconscionable time to cool his heels in the ante-chamber. Though his pieces had been set to music by such composers as Lawes, Ramsay, and Laniers, and his court poems had naturally won favor with the Cavalier party, Herrick cut but a small figure at the side of several of his rhyming contemporaries who are now forgotten. It sometimes happens that the light love-song, reaching few or no ears at its first singing, outlasts the seemingly more prosperous ode which, dealing with some passing phase of thought, social or political, gains the instant applause of the multitude. In most cases the timely ode is somehow apt to fade with the circumstance that inspired it, and becomes the yesterday's editorial of literature. Oblivion likes especially to get hold of occasional poems. That makes it hard for feeble poets laureate.

Mr. Henry James once characterized Alphonse Daudet as "a great little novelist." Robert Herrick is a great little poet. The brevity of his poems, for he wrote nothing *de longue haleine*, would place him among the minor singers; his workmanship places him among the masters. The Herricks were not a family of goldsmiths and lapidaries for nothing. The accurate touch of the artificer in jewels and costly metals was one of the gifts transmitted to Robert Herrick. Much of his work is as exquisite and precise as the chasing on a dagger-hilt by Cellini; the line has nearly always that vine-like fluency which seems impromptu, and is never the result of anything but austere labor. The critic who, borrowing Milton's words, described these carefully wrought poems as "wood-notes wild" showed a singular lapse of penetration. They are full of subtle simplicity. Here we come across a stanza as severely cut as an antique cameo — the stanza, for instance, in which the poet speaks of his lady-love's "winter face" — and there a couplet that breaks into unfading daffodils and violets. The art, though invisible, is always there. His amatory songs and catches are such poetry as Orlando would have liked to hang on the boughs in the forest of Arden. None of the work is hastily done, not even that portion of it we could wish had not been done at all. Be the motive grave or gay, it is given that faultlessness of form which distinguishes everything in literature that has survived its own period. There is no such thing as "form" alone; it is only the close-grained material that takes the highest finish. The structure of Herrick's verse, like that of Blake, is simple to the verge of innocence. Such rhythmic intricacies as those of Shelley, Tennyson, and Swinburne he never dreamed of. But his manner has this perfection: it fits his matter as the cup of the acorn fits its meat.

Of passion, in the deeper sense, Herrick has little or none. Here are no "tears from the depth of some divine despair," no probings into the tragic heart of man, no insight that goes much farther than the pathos of a cowslip on a maiden's grave. The tendrils of his verse reach up to the light, and love the warmer side of the garden wall. But the reader who does not detect the seriousness under the lightness misreads Herrick. Nearly all true poets have been wholesome and joyous singers. A pessimistic poet, like the poisonous ivy, is one of nature's sarcasms. In his own bright pastoral way Herrick must always remain unexcelled. His limitations are certainly narrow, but they leave him in the sunshine. Neither in his thought nor in his utterance is there any complexity;

both are as pellucid as a woodland pond, content to duplicate the osiers and ferns, and, by chance, the face of a girl straying near its crystal. His is no troubled stream in which large trout are caught. He must be accepted on his own terms.

The greatest poets have, with rare exceptions, been the most indebted to their predecessors or to their contemporaries. It has wittily been remarked that only mediocrity is ever wholly original. Impressionability is one of the conditions of the creative faculty: the sensitive mind is the only mind that invents. What the poet reads, sees, and feels, goes into his blood, and becomes an ingredient of his originality. The color of his thought instinctively blends itself with the color of its affinities. A writer's style, if it have distinction, is the outcome of a hundred styles.

Though a generous borrower of the ancients, Herrick appears to have been exceptionally free from the influence of contemporary minds. Here and there in his work are traces of his beloved Ben Jonson, or fleeting impressions of Fletcher, and in one instance a direct infringement on Suckling; but the sum of Herrick's obligations of this sort is inconsiderable.

This indifference to other writers of his time, this insularity, was doubtless his loss. The more exalted imagination of Vaughan or Marvell or Herbert might have taught him a deeper note than he sounded in his purely devotional poems. Milton, of course, moved in a sphere apart. Shakespeare, whose personality still haunted the clubs and taverns which Herrick frequented on his first going up to London, failed to lay any appreciable spell upon him. That great name, moreover, is a jewel which finds no setting in Herrick's rhyme. His general reticence relative to brother poets is extremely curious when we reflect on his penchant for addressing four-line epics to this or that individual. They were, in the main, obscure individuals, whose identity is scarcely worth establishing. His London life, at two different periods, brought him into contact with many of the celebrities of the day; but his verse has helped to confer immortality on very few of them. That his verse had the secret of conferring immortality was one of his unshaken convictions. Shakespeare had not a finer confidence when he wrote,

> Not marble nor the gilded monuments
> Of princes shall outlive this powerful rhyme,

than has Herrick whenever he speaks of his own poetry, and he is not by any means backward in speaking of it. It was the breath of his nostrils. Without his Muse those nineteen years in that dull, secluded Devonshire village would have been unendurable.

His poetry has the value and the defect of that seclusion. In spite, however, of his contracted horizon, there is great variety in Herrick's themes. Their scope cannot be stated so happily as he has stated it:

I sing of brooks, of blossoms, birds and bowers,
Of April, May, of June, and July-flowers;
I sing of May-poles, hock-carts, wassails, wakes,
Of bridegrooms, brides, and of their bridal-cakes;
I write of Youth, of Love, and have access
By these to sing of cleanly wantonness;
I sing of dews, of rains, and piece by piece
Of balm, of oil, of spice and ambergris;
I sing of times trans-shifting, and I write
How roses first came red and lilies white;
I write of groves, of twilights, and I sing
The Court of Mab, and of the Fairy King;
I write of Hell; I sing (and ever shall)
Of Heaven, and hope to have it after all.

Never was there so pretty a table of contents! When you open his book the breath of the English rural year fans your cheek; the pages seem to exhale wildwood and meadow smells, as if sprigs of tansy and lavender had been shut up in the volume and forgotten. One has a sense of hawthorn hedges and wide-spreading oaks, of open lead-set lattices half hidden with honeysuckle; and distant voices of the haymakers, returning home in the rosy afterglow, fall dreamily on one's ear, as sounds should fall when fancy listens. There is no English poet so thoroughly English as Herrick. He painted the country life of his own time as no other has painted it at any time.

It is to be remarked that the majority of English poets regarded as national have sought their chief inspiration in almost every land and period excepting their own. Shakespeare went to Italy, Denmark, Greece, Egypt, and to many a hitherto unfooted region of the imagination, for plot and character. It was not Whitehall Garden, but the Garden of Eden and the celestial spaces, that lured Milton. It is the "Ode on a Grecian Urn," "The Eve of St. Agnes," and the noble fragment of "Hyperion" that have given Keats his spacious niche in the gallery of English poets. Shelley's two masterpieces, "Prometheus Unbound" and "The Cenci," belong respectively to Greece and Italy. Browning's "The Ring and the Book" is Italian; Tennyson wandered to the land of myth for the "Idylls of the King," and Matthew Arnold's "Sohrab and Rustum"— a narrative poem second in dignity to none produced in the nineteenth century — is a Persian story. But Herrick's "golden apples" sprang from the soil in his own day, and reddened in the mist and sunshine of his native island.

Even the fairy poems, which must be classed

by themselves, are not wanting in local flavor. Herrick's fairy world is an immeasurable distance from that of "A Midsummer Night's Dream." Puck and Titania are of finer breath than Herrick's little folk, who may be said to have Devonshire manners and to live in a miniature England of their own. Like the magician who summons them from nowhere, they are fond of color and perfume and substantial feasts, and indulge in heavy draughts — from the cups of morning-glories. In the tiny sphere they inhabit, everything is marvelously adapted to their requirement; nothing is out of proportion or out of perspective. The elves are a strictly religious people in their winsome way, "part pagan, part papistical;" they have their pardons and indulgences, their psalters and chapels, and

> An apple's-core is hung up dried,
> With rattling kernels, which is rung
> To call to Morn and Even-song;

and very conveniently,

> Hard by, i' th' shell of half a nut,
> The Holy-water there is put.

It is all delightfully naïve and fanciful, this elfin-world, where the impossible does not strike one as incongruous, and the England of 1648 seems never very far away.

It is only among the apparently unpremeditated lyrical flights of the Elizabethan dramatists that one meets with anything like the lilt and liquid flow of Herrick's songs. While in no degree Shakespearian echoes, there are epithalamia and dirges of his that might properly have fallen from the lips of Posthumus in "Cymbeline." This delicate epicede would have fitted Imogen:

Here a solemne fast we keepe
While all beauty lyes asleepe;
Husht be all things; no noyse here
But the toning of a teare,
Or a sigh of such as bring
Cowslips for her covering.

Many of the pieces are purely dramatic in essence; the Mad Maid's Song, for example. The lyrist may speak in character, like the dramatist. A poet's lyrics may be, as most of Browning's are, just so many *dramatis personae.* "Enter a Song singing" is the stage direction in a seventeenth-century play whose name escapes me. The sentiment dramatized in a lyric is not necessarily a personal expression. In one of his couplets Herrick neatly denies that his more mercurial utterances are intended presentations of himself:

To his Book's end this last line he 'd have placed —
Jocund his Muse was, but his Life was chaste.

In point of fact he was a whole group of imaginary lovers in one. Silvia, Anthea, Electra,

Perilla, Perenna, and the rest of those lively ladies ending in *a*, were doubtless, for the most part, but airy phantoms dancing — as they should not have danced — through the brain of a sentimental old bachelor who happened to be a vicar of the Church of England. Even with his overplus of heart it would have been quite impossible for him to have had enough to go round had there been so numerous actual demands upon it.

Thus much may be conceded to Herrick's verse: at its best it has wings that carry it nearly as close to heaven's gate as any of Shakespeare's lark-like interludes. The brevity of the poems and their uniform smoothness sometimes produce the effect of monotony. The crowded richness of the line advises a desultory reading. But one must go back to them again and again. They bewitch the memory, having once caught it, and insist on saying themselves over and over. Among the poets of England the author of the "Hesperides" remains, and is likely to remain, unique. As Shakespeare stands alone in his vast domain, so Herrick stands alone in his scanty plot of ground.

Shine, Poet! in thy place, and be content.

A SEA TURN

AND OTHER MATTERS

A SEA TURN

I

Any one catching a casual glimpse of the Brandons in their summer cottage on Marblehead Neck would have inferred that the young couple were basking in the light of their honeymoon, though in point of fact that ineffable satellite had waxed and waned — if it ever had really waned — five years before. In front of the cottage was a small garden, with a profusion of clove-pinks, hollyhocks, and cinnamon-roses, through which tangle of color and perfume a shell-paved walk ran from the piazza steps to a gate opening on the rustic street. Every morning, at precisely the same hour, Mrs. Brandon, in a pretty breakfast gown of some bright-tinted material, might have been seen standing by the gate and waving good-by to Mr. Brandon on his way to the station. By means of a wireless telegraph, a supplementary kiss was exchanged between them just as he was vanishing round the corner. Then Mrs. Brandon fluttered up the garden walk, like one of the bayadere butterflies that haunted the place, and so into the house.

Mr. Brandon went to Boston each day by the 8.15 train, and returned on the noon express. Twice in the month, however, he was detained in the city until late in the afternoon. On these occasions the parting at the garden gate was especially loverlike, and the wireless telegraph was worked to its fullest capacity. The separation was too brief to entail any serious gloom, and their partings, if sometimes a little italicized, were nearly always as cheerful as their meetings.

But one July morning a cloud, the merest shadow of a cloud, seemed to rest upon their farewell for the day. There was an almost imperceptible dimness in the blue of Mrs. Brandon's eyes, and though a smile illuminated her features, it was a little on one side of the mouth, and had something perfunctory about it. The deflection of a thousandth part of an inch in the curve of the upper lip would have turned the smile into a pout. Mr. Brandon, as he lingered a moment at the gate, displayed the physiognomy of one not completely satisfied with himself. He had not gone more than three yards from the paling when he hesitated, and retraced his steps.

"The truth is, Helen," he said, "I don't like the Barter tribe."

"Tribe? What an expression! One would

imagine they wore war-paint, and went about flourishing tomahawks and scalping-knives. Fortunately, we have sat in their wigwam and smoked the pipe of peace with them."

"Yes, we 've eaten of their venison. I don't think it agreed with me."

"Why don't you like the Barters, Ned?"

"I don't know, and that makes me dislike them all the more. It 's a clear case of 'Dr. Fell.' They take their wealth so placidly; I suppose that 's it. They seem to me to have the unassuming arrogance of ample income."

"I wish we had it, dear — the income. I don't see anything arrogant in them. They strike me as straightforward, kindly people, and quite unspoiled by money. The Barters have been very polite to us. They are rich, and they live richly, and so would you and I, if we were in their place, and make a good deal more dash, too. There's no iniquity in keeping an expensive yacht, when one can afford it."

"And there's no harm in a neighbor taking an afternoon cruise in it, if she's invited. I'm sorry that I raised the slightest objection. I really don't care."

"But you said you did, and you do. You said the Barters were not the kind of persons you would prefer to see me intimate with, and they can't have reformed and become quite desirable acquaintances in the space of five minutes."

"Don't be a willful goose, Helen. It is I who have reformed. I can do it any time in two minutes. I 've done it repeatedly. The Barters are all right. Go and have your sail, dear."

"No, Ned; you give in to me because you are so good; but I know that down deep in your heart you disapprove of them—not of them really, but Mrs. Barter's brother. You can't forgive him for seeming to think me very nice at the regatta two weeks ago, and I 'm sure I was. He did n't do a thing but overfeed me with macaroons. Well, I give up the sail quite willingly. Your objection has taken the possible pleasure out of it."

"But I don't object."

"Oh, Ned! you will miss your train! You have n't a second to lose. There!—quick now."

As Mr. Brandon hurried away, he said, looking back over his shoulder: "I don't care two coppers about that hand-made dude—what 's-his-name?—Mitchell."

With the light chestnut hair blown about her face, and such indigo blue in her eyes as Neptune's daughter might have had, the young woman made a winsome picture lingering there by the fence under the elm boughs.

II

The composite smile still rested on Mrs. Brandon's lips as she reëntered the cottage and passed into the sitting-room. On a desk between two windows lay the note which had furnished the text for their breakfast-table talk that morning. Stamped at the top of the sheet was a tiny reproduction in colors of Commodore Barter's private yacht-signal. The note paper was obviously his, though it gave forth a faint breath of vervain and bore the penmanship of Mrs. Barter. Mrs. Brandon, with a half-unconscious sigh, picked up the epistle and read it again.

"It is just a family party," wrote Mrs. Barter; "there will be nobody but the Commodore, the two children, my brother, and myself. I learn that Mr. Brandon is to pass the day in town, or the invitation would eagerly include him. His absence, however, makes me feel more confident of securing you. Do come! The launch will be at the wharf at ten o'clock. I will meet you there or call for you, whichever you like. We promise to have you safely on shore in time to welcome Mr. Brandon by the 6.30 train — if that 's his train. You see I know your exemplary habits!"

Mrs. Brandon, with a complete sigh this time, replaced the note on the desk, and glanced wistfully out of the bay-window which overlooked the sea. It was a heavenly blue and gold day, following a week of rain. The breeze swayed the elm boughs in the old-fashioned garden and made white caps on the stretch of azure water glimpsed beyond. In the distance the sails of diminutive fishing-boats flashed in the sun like silver fins. At her moorings, half a mile from shore, lay the Barter yacht, rising and falling with the gentle swell as gracefully as a pond-lily. The busy black specks on the deck were sailors swinging out the boat-boom. Presently the quartermaster's whistle sent a faint bird-like trill through the air, and they could be seen lowering the naphtha launch from the davits. Then a sailor ran out on the slender boom, probably with the boat-cushions under one arm.

Mrs. Brandon turned away her eyes; she could not bear to look any more, such a sea-longing stirred in her bosom. Her gaze wandered idly round the room, and again rested by chance on Mrs. Barter's invitation lying on the desk. At that instant a mysterious flurry of wind lifted the half-folded sheet and dropped it at Helen Brandon's feet. She stooped and picked up the note. Her fingers no sooner touched the paper than she felt that the thing was hypnotizing her.

"I 've half a mind to go," she dreamily murmured to herself. "It was unreasonable for Edward to object in the first place. I shall be alone all day, and I think it very unkind of him to wish to deny me so innocent a pleasure, simply because he does n't happen to fancy Mrs. Barter's brother. It 's going to be dreadfully hot here, as well as in the city. Edward was obliged to go to town; that could n't be helped; but there 's no reason why I should suffer also. My being uncomfortable is n't likely to make it any cooler for him. Besides, I can get back by five or six o'clock, and he need n't know anything about it, though of course I shall tell him before he 's been home five minutes, — I 'm just that foolish where Ned is concerned, — and then he may scold as much as he wants to; I shall have had a delightful sail along the coast, and escaped the heat. Dear Ned! he 's as full of prejudices as he can hold; but I would n't have him changed in any particular. It would n't be the same Ned if he did n't have his little faults" — and Mrs. Brandon blew a condoning message to him through the air from the tips of her fingers.

Thus the innocent-looking missive, held lightly in her hand, had succeeded in working its occult spell. Helen seated herself at the desk, wrote a few lines accepting with pleasure

Mrs. Barter's "sweetest invitation," and dispatched them to their address by Mr. Peevey, the gardener.

On leaving the house an hour or so later, Mrs. Brandon did not confide her intended movements to Liza, the maid, but merely remarked:

"I am to lunch out, Liza, and shall probably not return before five or six o'clock — if any one calls."

III

When Edward Brandon reached his office that morning, he was not slightly vexed to learn that the afternoon business conference had been postponed — not that he was desirous of spending the entire day in the broiling city, but he had given up one or two pleasant schemes in order to do so. He was at liberty to return to Marblehead by the noon express, and he took his way to the North Station in no amiable mood. He had the peculiarity of not liking to have his plans disarranged, even when they were disagreeable. Once having resigned himself to the unpleasant, it was a waste of philosophic vitality not to face it. The purchasing of a bunch of violets at a florist's on Tremont Street was instrumental in partly restoring his good humor.

"It 's rather absurd of me," he reflected, "to grumble because I 've got an unexpected half holiday. I must have turned out wrong side up this morning. I did n't mean not to be nice to Nelly about the Barters. They 're well enough, I dare say, but old Barter — I don't know why I call him old Barter, for he is not more than seven years my senior — somehow always gets on my nerves with his blue yachting cap and red nose and salty manner generally. However, I can stand the Commodore, but that brother of Mrs. Barter, with his talk about 'the Venus de Medici' and 'the Uffizi Gallery at Florence' (as if it could be anywhere else!) is a horror. . . . Nelly will be surprised to see me back so soon. After lunch we 'll drive over to Gloucester and call on the Bellamys. They are certain to keep us to dinner, and the ride home in the moonlight will be charming."

Brandon had hardly seated himself on the shady side of the crowded Pullman when three young men entered the car — three excellent specimens of elegant Young Boston. Their athletic figures and bronzed faces told of polo and golf and sea weather. One of the three had the remains of a rich tan lately caught in the trenches before Santiago. The trio were clad in blue flannel suits, and might have been taken for naval officers in mufti. They were respectively known to their prosperous world, and perhaps beyond, as Morton Bangs, John Beverly, and Peabody Preston.

"There's Brandon now!" cried Mr. Bangs, the knight of the copper countenance. "We have just looked in at your office to ask you to take a spin with us. The yacht's at Marblehead."

"What's the Spitfire doing at Marblehead?" asked Brandon, giving a hand to each of the three graces in turn.

"We scuttled in there out of the wet the other night, and I ran up to town by rail. Preston and I are to lunch with Beverly at the club, and then we are going to try our new jibs and topsails. We got blown to ribbons Friday night off Cape Ann. Won't you come along?"

"I wish I could, Bangs, but I am to drive Mrs. Brandon over to Gloucester, where we have a sort of engagement to dine with the Bellamys."

"Devilish sorry, — with kindest regards to Mrs. Brandon all the same. Could n't we run into Gloucester — there'll be a moon, you know — and bring the pair of you back to Marblehead?"

"Carriage and all?"

"Confound the carriage! — leave it," suggested Preston.

"I could n't do that."

Brandon was both glad and sorry to have so good an excuse for declining the invitation. The Spitfire was the fastest yacht of her class in the Eastern Squadron, and it was always a pleasure to be on her; but the Spitfire — were one to give heed to envious talk — was no faster than her owner. Now, if Commodore Barter was Mr. Brandon's *bête noire*, Morton Bangs was Mrs. Brandon's, and in view of the conversation with Helen that morning, it struck Edward as diplomatic, on the present occasion, at least, to respect her deplorable prejudice. Moreover, he preferred to spend the day with his wife.

"If this wind holds," said Morton Bangs, as the train slowed up and stopped in the Marblehead station, "we shall have a blooming spin. I 'm awfully sorry, my boy, you can't come. Should Madam have a headache, or anything change your plans, you 'll find the gig at the landing at two o'clock sharp. If you 're a bit late, give us a whistle. We shan't get off immediately. Don't intend to be out over five or six hours. God go with you, Señor, as they say down in Cuba, and usually mean quite a different accompaniment."

Edward Brandon could not justify to himself his sense of personal grievance on not finding Helen at the cottage. Why should she have remained at home? It was only natural that she should not care to eat her lunch alone and mope the rest of the day in solitude. She had left no word for him, — of course she had n't, — not expecting him back until after seven. Yet, in spite of his reasoning, he vaguely resented Helen's absence.

"Did n't say where she was going, Liza?"

"No, sir; she only said she should n't be in for the afternoon."

There were a dozen places along the North Shore to which Helen might have been invited unceremoniously. She had had no engagement when he quitted her. Somebody had dropped in by chance, and seeing his wife alone, had asked her to lunch. It was plainly an impromptu affair.

"Did they come in a carriage, Liza?"

"Who, sir?"

"The persons who took Mrs. Brandon away."

"Nobody took her, sir. She did n't go in a carriage. She walked."

Then Helen must have gone to some place in the immediate neighborhood. Edward wondered where; but he had no intention of looking her up, with so many chances against finding her. The day was a failure from beginning to end, and there was nothing to do but to take the matter philosophically. A book and a cigar, and perhaps a stroll by the water-side, would help kill time until she came home. A glimmering consciousness of how dependent he was on Helen came over him.

"Tell Susan to cook a chop for me, Liza, or send up a slice of cold ham, or something — I don't care what. If there 's a bottle of Bass on the ice, serve that."

"Yes, sir."

Mr. Brandon was on the point of sitting down to his silent meal when the Spitfire swept into his mind and dropped anchor, so to speak.

"By Jove!" he exclaimed, pushing away the empty plate in front of him, "I was n't due before 7.30, anyhow. There 's no use in my mooning about the house all the afternoon. The boys can't have finished tiffin yet — maybe they have n't begun. I 'll join them. Nothing but a dash of blue water will cure me of my dumps. If I don't get back at precisely 7.30 — why, the train was n't on time. It is n't necessary to bother Nelly about it. I am sorry she does n't like Morton Bangs. What a breeze for the Spitfire!"

It is to be noticed that the husband's conscience was an easier working piece of mechanism than the wife's. Hastily snatching up a light overcoat from the hat-rack in the hall, Mr. Brandon started for the front door.

"By the way, Liza, I was n't expected back until evening, and you need n't say anything about me when Mrs. Brandon returns. It would only make her sorry that she went out."

"I wonder what 's up, I do," was the comment of Liza, the maid, standing by the parlor window. "He has n't touched a mouthful of food. The cook 'll be mad, that 's one comfort. I wonder why cooks are always so very crusty. I suppose they get overdone. The mistress being away seems to have upset Mr. B. She went off queerly, I must say. There 's something gone wrong, more 's the pity, and the two just like a pair of cooing doves on a roof ever since I 've been in the place."

IV

Veuve Clicquot in the middle of the day is perhaps not quite good form, but it is wholly palatable, and deviled crab, like Mr. Emerson's rhodora, is always its own excuse for being. Helen Brandon pronounced the lunch delicious, exquisitely prepared and served; and, indeed, Commodore Barter's chef was worth his weight in truffles. The invigorating salt air had given everybody an appetite. The two little Barters had to have sandwiches applied to them before the Pelican was well out of the harbor.

As Mrs. Brandon sat in a bamboo chair near

the companion-hatch, with the mainsail looming above her like a vast snowy cloud, it was to be seen that her face had lost the touch of pensiveness which had marked it when she came aboard. Mrs. Barter had been very sweet and matronly with her, and the Commodore, in his bluff, hearty fashion, had been charming. He was a short gentleman, inclined to stoutness, with grayish hair and florid complexion, and a more prominent nose than perhaps he himself would have chosen had he been consulted in the matter; but not at all an ill-looking person. It was too bad of Edward to liken him to the carving on Baron Puck's umbrella handle in "La Grande Duchesse." But that was Edward's wicked way. And Mr. Mitchell, Mrs. Barter's brother, he was not in the least a dude. He had spent much time abroad, and if something in America was always reminding him — or not reminding him — of something on the Continent, where was the harm? One must expect to be bored a little by persons who have traveled.

For Mrs. Brandon Mr. Mitchell's absence would really have been a partial eclipse of the promised gayety. It was so amusing to watch how fate led him, fatuitous and unconscious, into the trap of foreign reminiscence. Mrs. Brandon waited in tingling expectancy for the inevitable appearance of "the Venus de Medici;" and it was only after a stroll through "the Uffizi Gallery at Florence" that she settled herself down to the tranquil enjoyment of the occasion.

The town of Marblehead, with its weather-stained roofs and spires, had long since crumbled on the horizon, and now lay sunken in the sea like some fabulous city of old. Presently there was nothing to be seen but sky and ocean, with here and there a spectral sail, or a coastwise steamer leaving a trail of black smoke against the blue. With what grace the Pelican dipped and rose, shaking the white crystals from her beak! Mrs. Brandon had come of a breed of sailors, and there was true sea in her blood. The sense of space and the contagious exhilaration in the air added a color to her cheeks as she sat there, looking supremely content, save at intervals, when her thought reverted to dear Edward sweltering in his stuffy office on Court Street — bending fagged at his desk in a mephitic odor of calf-skin and Russia leather, instead of facing these heavenly breezes and drinking in all this invisible liquid silver. Poor dear Edward!

Mr. Mitchell, who had been assiduous in fetching wraps and footstools for the two ladies, was standing at Mrs. Brandon's side with a glass at his eye intently inspecting some object in the distance. After a minute or two he lowered the glass, and said:

"That 's the Spitfire—Morton Bangs's boat. She seems to be heading for Boston."

(At the same instant, as it happened, Morton Bangs turned to Edward Brandon and remarked:

"The Commodore's flag over yonder."

"Yes, I knew he was to take a run this afternoon. He invited my wife, but she could n't go."

"Quaint old boy — Lemuel Barter."

"Very. Ought to have been born in the seventeenth century. *I* don't want him.")

"Is Mr. Bangs a friend of yours, Mr. Mitchell?" asked Mrs. Brandon, looking up.

"Oh, Bangs is everybody's friend; he 's very popular. He and I were in Switzerland together two summers ago. We had quite a thrilling adventure in the Simplon Pass. Our *vetturino*, a Piedmontese named Martelli, got grossly intoxicated one day, and" — here Mr. Mitchell, detecting a lack of breathless interest in Mrs. Brandon's expression, adroitly brought his narrative to a close by saying, "and Bangs behaved in the pluckiest manner. Don't you know him?"

"My husband is acquainted with him. I know

Mr. Bangs only slightly. He is rather fast, is n't he?"

"Nautically or personally?"

"Personally."

"Well, no, I don't think so," replied Mr. Mitchell. "He is not slow. He's an agreeable fellow, and a most delightful host on the water. His yachting parties are always lively."

"So I have heard," said Mrs. Brandon.

The two yachts were now dipping their colors, and the conversation ended.

For the last hour or more the breeze had gradually lessened, and though the Pelican from time to time made one of those plunges which, aided by too much fruit cake, had eliminated the two small Barters from general society, it was only a half-hearted plunge. The vessel was gliding on a comparatively level keel. The gentler motion was provocative of reverie, and Mrs. Brandon yielded herself up to it unresistingly. She did not care to talk, and when Mr. Mitchell retreated to a camp-stool on the other side of the deck, she scarcely noticed the movement. Mrs. Barter was below with the children, the Commodore had gone to the chart-room, and Helen was left alone to her sea-dreams. With partly closed eyes she leaned back on the cushions. After awhile she was aroused by the Commodore's voice.

"That certainly looks like fog, Captain Jones, but I don't think it will amount to much. You can keep on our course, and go about just before we come to Thatcher's Island. There 'll be time enough to get back."

Then Mrs. Brandon drifted off into a delicious drowse again, a semi-conscious trance in which she had the sensation of floating through interminable stretches of gray and silvery clouds. Faint, elusive shore-scents, as if blown from groves of lemon and magnolia, now and then touched her nostrils, and set her dreaming of the tropics. That penciled streak of vapor lying against the horizon, which she occasionally glimpsed through her drooping eyelashes, might have been Jamaica or a bit of the Haytian coast-line. How long this lasted she could not tell, when something caused her to sit bolt upright in her chair. The boat was making so slight headway as to seem almost stationary. The day had strangely darkened. A thick haze enveloped everything. The faint, melancholy throb of a bell came from across the water.

"The wind is leaving us entirely, sir," the Captain was saying.

"And the fog seems to be closing in. Can't we manage to make a harbor, Captain?"

"I 'm afraid not, sir, with this wind. It 's almost gone, sir."

"Then we shall have to lie here all night."

"You don't mean it!" cried Mrs. Brandon, springing to her feet.

"Unfortunately it looks that way," said the Commodore.

"But I can't stay aboard this yacht the entire night!" cried Mrs. Brandon, pressing one hand against her bosom and white with agitation. "I — I — the inconvenience, the" —

"You need n't worry over that, my dear lady; Mrs. Barter and I can make you very comfortable."

Comfortable! — and Edward not knowing where she was and going crazy about her! Comfortable! Oh, why did she disregard his wishes, almost positively disobeying him! Would he ever forgive her? How could she explain it to him! And Mr. Mitchell! It was particularly awkward having him on board. He had been polite with his wraps and apollinaris and things, and had not once passed the limit of mere politeness; but if Mrs. Brandon could have had her will this moment, she would have fed that innocent gentleman over the side to the sharks. He was the only person who had ever stirred the slightest grain of jealousy in Edward, and there were a dozen other men she had liked ten times as well. It appeared as if the hand of destiny out of pure malice had selected him as the instrument with which to punish her.

What would Edward think had become of her? She had covered up her tracks like a criminal, as she was. If it occurred to him to go to the Barter mansion for information, he would get none, for she had gone directly from the cottage to the boat-landing, and met nobody. It would soon be time for Edward to take his train. She pictured his arrival, his surprise, his increasing anxiety, and then his despair. She saw him, with men and lanterns in wherries, searching the water-front throughout the livelong coming night. The adjacent woodlands would be ransacked; the whole neighborhood would be discussing her unaccountable disappearance.

Helen cast a terrified look around her. The fog was shutting down in every direction. The only objects visible were two phantomish lighthouses on Thatcher's Island in the distance, and they were rapidly dissolving. An unseen bell-buoy, somewhere, kept up its dismal iteration.

With a gasp of dismay Mrs. Brandon sank down in the bamboo chair, where she sat until it was too damp for her to remain longer on deck. At dinner she made heroic attempts to join in the conversation and mask her anguish, the uncomplimentary nature of which could not be revealed to the Barters. They must not suspect that her husband had opposed her acceptance of their invitation and was wholly unaware that she had accepted it. How could she tell them that? The cook had surpassed himself on the menu; but the fabrics of his skill lay untasted on her plate. A thimbleful of sherry was all she could swallow.

As soon as the gentlemen took to their cigars, Mrs. Brandon pleaded a headache and retired to the small cabin assigned her. Kneeling on the locker, and with one cheek pressed against the open port, she tried to pierce the pallid darkness that surrounded them. The twin lights on Thatcher's Island, like a pair of eyes blurred with grief, were just distinguishable through the gloom. While she was watching them the faintly luminous spots faded out, and the fog wrapped the becalmed vessel in a great black pall of velvet. Not a breath stirred the stagnant air, and the motionless water lay as smooth as oil.

"What shall I say to him to-morrow — if to-morrow ever comes?" was Mrs. Brandon's agonized reflection. "He will not have gone to town, of course. Having perhaps spent the entire night walking up and down the room, he will be waiting for some tidings of me. If the Barters were alone concerned, it would be bad enough; but how can I make Edward understand that Mr. Mitchell had nothing whatever to do with my going on the excursion—that not so much as a thought of the man ever entered my head? And Edward is so sensible on every other subject. What a delightful meeting that will be to-morrow!" and she immediately fell to dramatizing it. With a sudden little shudder she fancied herself opening the garden gate in the broad daylight and wearily dragging her feet up the piazza steps—like a returned repentant wife terrified at the thought of her probable reception. Then she tried to imagine a happier dénouement, Edward's wild joy at holding her in his arms again — but here her invention somehow flagged and failed.

Finally Helen threw herself, partly disrobed, on the narrow berth; but not to sleep. Throughout the endless night she heard the ship's bell strike the hours and half hours.

V

"I rather guess we are in for it," said Morton Bangs, removing the beaded moisture from his cap by striking it smartly against the taffrail. "This fog means business."

"Business," repeated Edward Brandon, in a tone of deep disgust; "what in the deuce do you mean by business?"

"I intended to intimate that it has come to stay."

"For how long, do you think?" Brandon asked anxiously.

"As long as it pleases. I've known a fog of this complexion to last two or three days. But one can never know. Maybe it will lift by the next tide, and maybe it will hold on until daybreak."

"The devil!"

A colloquy similar in essence, though different in form, had taken place somewhat earlier in the afternoon on the deck of the Pelican.

"What's the correct time?" inquired Preston.

"It will be two bells in a minute," said Beverly, looking at his watch.

"Where are we, anyhow?"

"Well, we are nowhere in particular," observed Bangs cheerfully. Lynn is over there in some direction. I sighted Egg Rock on the port bow just before the fog got its back up."

"Can't we run into Lynn Harbor?" asked Brandon, "or Swampscott, or some other infernal place?"

"Some other infernal place, maybe," answered Bangs, "but not Lynn Harbor."

"Can't we, can't we?" cried Brandon, whose face had grown sharp and pallid within the last half hour.

"My boy," said Morton Bangs, "the wind 's as dead as Julius Cæsar."

"But I 've got to be home by 7.30!"

"'Be it ever so humble, there 's no place like home,'"

hummed Beverly, with an instinct for appropriate music.

"If you 're in a great hurry, Brandon," said Bangs, "perhaps you had better get out and walk."

"Steward," Preston shouted down the hatchway, "Mr. Brandon's overshoes!"

This levity so little harmonized with Brandon's unhappy frame of mind that he turned his shoulder on the group and went forward.

"What will Nelly say to me?" he muttered. "How will she take it? I can fancy! I vow I shall actually be afraid to face her to-morrow morning. Her disapproval of me, even in a slight matter, is a thing I can't stand. I may put on superior airs and carry my nose as high as I will, but there 's no disguising the fact that I 'm tied to the apron-string of that dear woman."

The sudden rush of anchor-chains, followed by the vicious plunge of the anchor, interrupted him for a few seconds. A dense white fog, like a wall, had now shut them off from the rest of the world.

"She will have just cause to reproach me,"

Brandon went on, in his meditation; "my thoughtlessness was simply cruel. She can't of course have the dimmest idea of my whereabouts. Her first thought will be that I 've tumbled into the harbor, and she 's entirely capable of setting the drag-nets at work. Why did n't I have the manhood to tell Liza where I was going? Then this cursed fog would have explained my detention, and though Nelly might have worried more or less, she would n't have been torn to pieces by every horrible conjecture. I am not worthy of her; she ought to be glad to have me disappear permanently. I wonder what she is up to now. If she 's fretting about me as I 'm fretting about her, the poor child is not having a good time. Not one of the boys here has any more heart than a brickbat. I 've told them that my wife does n't know I 'm off yachting, and they seem to think the situation facetious." At this point Brandon paused, and sent a scowl aft, where his shipmates were chatting and laughing unconcernedly. "When I listen to those fellows, I begin to understand what a holy joy it must be to a mob now and then to destroy a man and a brother."

"Brandon, my dear boy," cried Preston, "this will never do. You look like the Ancient Mariner after he 'd eaten the canary — I mean after he 'd shot the albatross. Cheer up!"

"Peabody Preston, if I had been the Ancient Mariner, and you had been a passenger on board that ship, it is n't the albatross that would have got killed."

"Of course not — you'd have missed the bird and hit one of the crew. I know how you shoot. No man's life would have been safe an instant, — except when you were aiming at him. Oh, you need n't explain! I understood your bloodthirsty insinuation."

Brandon cast a homicidal look on the speaker, and then turning away stood and glared at the fog.

It was very merry in the cabin that night, with bright talk at dinner, and afterward over the cigars and coffee; but nothing could dispel Edward Brandon's gloom. It was impossible to laugh him or chaff him out of his dejection, and benevolent efforts to that end were not wanting on the part of his companions. There seemed to Brandon a demoniacal note in their hilarity. He turned in early, and lay in his bunk sleepless, smoking incalculable cigarettes. Somewhere towards midnight he called out:

"I wish to the Lord that somebody would n't bang that bell every two minutes!"

"Silence that dreadful bell!" cried Beverly, throwing himself into the attitude of the Moor of Venice; "it frights the yacht from her propriety."

Brandon got up and slammed to his door, which had sprung open. It was not until the lantern in the forerigging began to pale in the dawn that the wretched man fell asleep.

VI

Liza sat up until nearly twelve o'clock that night, awaiting the return of her master and mistress, and then went to bed in a state of wonderment. In the same state of wonderment she was mechanically laying the breakfast-table the next morning, when Mrs. Brandon walked into the dining-room. There were dark circles under her eyes, and her manner betrayed suppressed agitation. She had a hundred questions to put to Liza, but only one rose to Helen's lips as she hurriedly threw aside her wraps:

"Has Mr. Brandon come down yet, Liza?"

Now Mr. Brandon had always been especially pleasant with Liza, and, to use her own phrasing of it, she was not going to give him away; so she replied very demurely:

"No, ma'am;" but the girl had no sooner spoken the words than she caught her breath, and added, "Yes, ma'am. I did n't know he had left his room. He 's in the garden, ma'am."

Helen glanced through the window and saw her husband leisurely shutting the gate behind him, as if he had just returned from one of his eccentric morning strolls. He carried a light overcoat on his arm, a circumstance that did not impress her, for there was always a chill in the early day at the seaside. Mr. Brandon halted abstractedly halfway up the walk, and pulled a rose from an overhanging bush.

When Mr. Brandon entered the room his wife was seated at the coffee-urn and in the act of reaching out one hand to take a cup from the tray. There was a wan, tentative smile on her face as she lifted the fatigued blue eyes, and said:

"Good-morning, dear!"

The reception was so vastly different from anything he had expected as to stagger him for a second or two, until he reflected that of course Helen was not going to make a scene in the presence of the servant. She was too proud and too tactful for that. It was a piece of comedy on the part of his wife, — a bit of that adroit acting in which women excel; and he gratefully accepted the situation. He crossed over to her chair, and, laying the rose beside Helen's plate, stooped down and kissed her as usual. She shot a swift sideway glance at him from under her lashes, and foreboded the storm that lay behind all that assumed composure.

The breakfast proceeded as on ordinary mornings, except that both were unwontedly silent and preoccupied. The unavoidable explanation pressed heavily upon them. Every instant Edward was expecting that Liza would be dismissed, and then he should catch it! But nothing was farther from Helen's desire than to be left alone, just yet, with her husband. Liza was quick enough to perceive this, and lent herself to the sundry little stratagems employed to detain her.

The girl, meanwhile, was dying with curiosity and perplexity. The master and mistress had spent the night away, and neither appeared to be aware that the other had done so. They had quitted the house separately, and returned separately. What did it mean? Liza in her time had assisted at various domestic dramas, but nothing resembling this.

One seemingly perilous interval occurred near the close of the meal, when Liza was summoned from the room by a ring at the door-bell. "Now he's going to speak!" said Helen to herself, with a tremor. "Here's her opportunity!" thought Edward. But nothing happened, to their mutual surprise and relief.

The breakfast was late, and had scarcely come

to an end when it was time for Mr. Brandon to take his train to Boston. A momentary panic seized both husband and wife at the prospect of those one or two minutes alone together at the garden gate; but the reflection that the spot was of all spots the least adapted to a family discussion reassured them.

The parting took place, a more hurried parting than customary, and neither had spoken of what lay nearest to their hearts. Mr. Brandon went to town wondering at Helen's singular forbearance, while Helen began to feel a chill creeping over her as she reflected on Edward's suppression of his just displeasure. Her transgression had been very great, — every moment it seemed to her less and less forgivable, — and he had treated the matter with cold indifference. He no longer loved her! They were joining, or had already joined, that long procession of piteous couples who keep up the outside semblance of marriage, having really nothing left but the thin shell of vanished happiness.

On reëntering the house, Mrs. Brandon called Liza into the parlor.

"Liza," she said, "I am in very great trouble. Unfortunately I did not let Mr. Brandon know yesterday that I was going with Mr. and Mrs. Barter for a short sail in their yacht. We got caught in a fog and were unable to reach land until seven o'clock this morning. I am afraid Mr. Brandon is very angry with me, so angry that he has not trusted himself to speak to me on the subject. What happened yesterday? What did he say when he returned home?"

"He asked where you had gone, ma'am, and I told him I did n't know. Then he asked who came and took you away, and I told him nobody."

"Was he not much surprised and disturbed?"

"He did n't seem quite pleased, ma'am."

"Pleased! What else did he say?"

"He did n't say anything else."

"You mean that that was *all* he said?"

"Yes, ma'am. Then he went out quite sudden like."

"In search of me," was Helen's mental comment. "And when he returned?"

"He dined out, ma'am—at least, he did n't have dinner here."

"In the course of the evening, before you went to bed, did he make any remark about my absence?"

"I did n't hear him make any remark," replied Liza, with the soul of truth looking through her gray eyes.

"Did n't he—did n't you hear him walking the floor, or moving around, or something, during the night?"

"No, ma'am," said the girl, who had all she could do to bite off the smile that was nibbling at the corners of her mouth.

"And when he came down this morning?"

"I didn't see him, ma'am, as you know. He was standing in the garden when I saw him first."

"Did he sit up very late last night?"

"I'm not sure, ma'am, but I think so. He looked it just now," added Liza, who was growing restless.

"And this is absolutely everything you have to tell me?"

"Yes, ma'am."

"Then it was scarcely worth while to question you. That will do, Liza. You certainly are a most observing girl."

"Yes, ma'am."

Any sarcasm not of the coarsest fibre was quite wasted on Liza.

The coolness with which her husband had seemed to accept her unexplained disappearance mystified and appalled Helen. It did not appear that he had scoured the water-front much, or ransacked the woodlands extensively on her account. Even if he had suspected, or in some way ascertained, where she was, a slight show of interest would have been becoming in him. Liza's report was inadequate, and presumably inaccurate. There was a nameless something in the girl's manner that vexed Mrs. Brandon, and her vexation was farther increased during the forenoon by the fancy that she detected from time to time a curious, sphinx-like expression on Liza's face. Could it be possible that the girl, who had been made much of by both Mr. Brandon and herself, and perhaps a little spoiled, was daring for an instant to sit in judgment on what had occurred? "No, my nerves are all broken up," thought Helen, "and I am just imagining that she looks at me strangely. Now she is doing it again!"

Mr. Brandon came home on the noon express. The lunch was marked by the same reticence and embarrassment as the morning repast. Each waited for the other to open fire from a hitherto masked battery, but neither made any demonstration.

It was one of Mrs. Brandon's Wednesdays, when a number of outlying friends and acquaintances always dropped in to take a cup of tea with her. Mr. Brandon was seldom in evidence at these functions, and this day he took himself off earlier than usual, with no word of notice to Helen, who was engaged in a forlorn fashion in preparing for her guests. She had been very unhappy that night on the Pelican, but her unhappiness, compared with the present state of suspense, began to fade out in the recollecting. Why did he not call her to an account for what she had done? Why this inexplicable silence? Was he waiting for her to come to him and implore his pardon? She was ready to do that now, if he would but give the slightest sign that such was his desire. He had made no such sign. His care-drawn face showed that he had suffered, or was suffering, a great strain. No amount of self-control could hide that. As Edward Brandon went down the piazza steps, Helen stood in the middle of the sitting-room and impulsively reached out her arms, as if to bring him back. But he was gone.

Mr. Brandon wandered over to the Eastern Yacht Club in a very dejected mood. Helen had not reproached him even by a look for his unfeeling treatment of her, and this angelic patience was becoming a heavier punishment to him than any angry word could have inflicted. From the moment he met Helen at breakfast until now, he had been in purgatory. A more advanced stage of expiation was becoming almost preferable. It was not possible to bear it much longer. He resolved to go and beg her forgiveness the moment that stupid tea business was over. She evidently had already forgiven him, like the seraph she was, but he wanted to hear her tell him so. How pale the dear girl looked at breakfast and lunch, and how bravely she hid the hurt, like — what was his name? — the Spartan boy with the fox tucked under his tunic.

Then his point of view abruptly changed, and the rose color faded out. Perhaps Helen's composure was the expression of complete estrangement and implacable disdain. His staying away all night would naturally have alarmed her, and his return ought to have lifted a heavy load from her heart; but she had ignored the whole business in a fashion that was simply blood-curdling.

"I'll be hanged if I understand it," Brandon said to himself. "I wish I could get hold of Liza alone for five or ten minutes; but the minx seems to keep out of my way on purpose. I'd like to know exactly what Nelly said and did last night. It would give me a clew to the actual state of her mind and be a help. I don't see how I am going to explain my utter thoughtlessness. I haven't the ghost of an excuse, and I shall be sure to say the wrong thing; I always do. Perhaps I had better write what I have to say. I'll do it this very instant, and send it over to the cottage by messenger. Maybe it will make the rest of the afternoon happier for her."

He was standing in the reading-room of the club-house when this expedient occurred to him. In the apartment were several desks amply furnished with stationery. Edward seated himself at the one nearest at hand and proceeded with much deliberation to select a stub-pen.

"I wish the note-paper did n't have the club's burgee stuck up in the corner — it's altogether too suggestive; but it can't be helped;" and he began writing:

Eastern Yacht Club.
Marblehead. Mass.

My dear girl:

When I married you five years ago, I more than half suspected that I was marrying an angel, and now I am positive of it. I can never forgive myself for the anxiety and suffering I must have caused you last night, and your divine sweetness in not upbraiding me with it is something I shall ever

"I beg pardon for interrupting you, Mr. Brandon," said Commodore Barter, approaching from the other end of the room, "but I wish to say how very sorry I am that we were obliged to keep Mrs. Brandon a prisoner all night. That devilish fog was unfortunate. But you're an old yachtsman, you understand these mishaps, and I trust that your wife's prolonged absence did n't give you too much uneasiness."

Brandon dropped his pen, and stared at the Commodore.

So Helen had gone with the Barters, after all — had been away the whole night! The same fog that had nipped him had nipped her! Talk about the hand of Providence! Was it possible that she was ignorant of his own little adventure, as he had been ignorant of hers? It was absolutely certain — unless Liza had chattered, which she did not appear to have done. No wonder Helen had n't pitched into him!

"Don't mention it, Commodore!" cried Brandon, rising quickly from his chair and wringing the elder man's hand with a cordiality that slightly surprised him. "I knew that my wife was perfectly safe with you."

If Edward Brandon was ever glad of anything in his life, it was of Helen's deceitful behavior. He had to shake hands again with the Commodore before that gentleman departed, and could have passed the remainder of the day pleasantly in that manual exercise. Had Mr.

Mitchell appeared at this instant with "the Venus de Medici" hanging on his arm, Edward Brandon would have slapped him on the back and invited the pair to champagne.

Presently Brandon tore his half-completed note into minute pieces, which he sifted into the waste-paper basket. Descending from the club-house veranda to the seaward-facing lawn, where he halted a few seconds to light a cigar, he treated himself to the following reflections:

"I'll just loaf round here until Nelly has scattered her tea leaves. It's as clear as day she does n't dream of the scrape *I* got into last night, and I don't see why I should n't have a bit of fun with her before she discovers it. I'll be very indignant and deeply hurt, and accuse her of coquetting indecorously with Barter's brother-in-law. I'll make a strong point of that. Come to think of it," — here he paused and snipped off his cigar-ash a trifle impatiently, — "that fellow Mitchell is a public nuisance. I don't want to do him injustice, but he seems to me to have all the symptoms of an ass. Nelly knew very well that he was to be of the party, and a little serious talking to — but, confound it! what shall I have to say by and by touching the Spitfire transaction? That's a bad handicap for me. What in the devil possessed me to set foot in that old tub, anyway! Perhaps

I had better drop Mitchell, and stick to the main issue. It will be more dignified. In going with Bangs I did n't deceive Nelly; in going with the Barters after pretending to refuse their invitation, she did deceive me. The two cases are not in the least analogous."

Mr. Brandon continued to pace up and down the lawn, pursuing this masculine train of reasoning, until his cigar was finished; then he returned to the reading-room and occupied himself by looking over the magazines for August.

Mrs. Brandon's supposed last caller had come and gone, and she was sitting meditatively on an ottoman near the fireplace, when Liza appeared at the parlor door and announced —

"Mr. Morton Bangs."

"My dear madam," said Mr. Bangs, advancing towards her in his confident breezy manner, "I come to lay my apologies at your feet. I cannot sufficiently express my regret for what happened. I did n't mean to keep your husband out all night."

"All night!"

"Well, practically all night. The fog did n't leave us until five o'clock this morning, when we made directly for Lynn Harbor. I never saw a man in such a state of mind. At one time, I assure you, I thought that Brandon was going to try to swim ashore. I don't believe

I shall ever get him on board the Spitfire again."

"My husband was on the Spitfire yesterday?"

"What! did n't you know?" gasped Mr. Bangs, with a chilling impression that he was somehow putting his foot into it.

"I knew he was somewhere, but not just where."

"Has n't he told you about it?"

"Mr. Brandon went to town by the early train this morning," said Mrs. Brandon, completely recovering herself, "and he had no opportunity to tell me any of the particulars of his outing. The pleasure of hearing those interesting details is still in store for me," and such a radiant smile broke over her face as seemed to fill the whole dingy little parlor with bloom. "Won't you let me give you a cup of tea, Mr. Bangs?"

"Thanks, awfully. I want to say again that Brandon was deeply distressed — we all were deeply distressed," he added shamelessly, "at the thought of the anxiety he was occasioning you."

"I was, indeed, very anxious last night."

"So sorry, Mrs. Brandon."

"It was not your fault, Mr. Bangs," said Helen magnanimously.

"So kind! It was n't Brandon's, either.

The fog did it all. When we met him coming down on the noon train" —

"The noon train!" Helen repeated to herself, and the perplexity went up into her eyebrows. "Why did n't Liza tell her that?"

— "Brandon flatly refused to go with us: but just as we were taking a — some apollinaris before lunch he dropped into the club and said he had changed his programme. Of course we were glad, he 's such delightful, animating company; but we were sorry enough afterward. The state of that youth when we got becalmed off Egg Rock (*he* did n't get becalmed!), and the language he used — only one lump, dear lady."

Mrs. Brandon was oblivious of the exact moment when Mr. Morton Bangs took his leave. The room was too small and hot to hold her; she could not breathe indoors. Pushing aside the portière which draped one of the windows, she stepped out on the piazza. The cool air revived her and gave her a chance to think a little. Edward had evidently returned home earlier than he expected, and finding her absent, had gone off with Mr. Bangs and his horrid friends and got befogged on the Spitfire, just as she had got befogged on the Pelican. And here the two of them had been going about in deadly fear of each other, neither having the faintest suspicion of the other's reprehensible conduct. Was there ever anything so deliciously absurd! If no one had told Edward — and who was to tell him? — he was still in the dark relative to her, and she decided to make a little scene when he came home. Her nerves had been at such a tension ever since yesterday afternoon that a few honest tears would be easy to shed. And had n't Edward been expecting them!

This idea was passing through Helen's brain when she saw her husband come swinging down the street with an elasticity of gait that had been a lost art to him for the last twelve or fourteen hours. He came smiling along the shell-paved walk, and stood in front of her. Then Helen's malicious plan instantly fell to pieces, for she saw by his face that he knew, and he saw that she knew, and with a great laugh, to which Helen added a merry contralto, Edward sprang up the piazza steps and took her in his arms.

Any one passing the cottage at the moment would have been dead certain that it was a honeymoon.

HIS GRACE THE DUKE

HAS the Duke of Suffolk no friends? If an English duke is without friends, or what pass for such, who on this earth can expect to have any? An English duke is a very great personage, — even to democracy on this side the water. Our most reluctant doors turn quickly on their hinges at his faintest knock. If he chance to occupy our guest-room for a night, a glamour hangs over the apartment forever. We sow bitterness in the heart of Mrs. Leo Hunter by incidentally remarking, "Yes; this is where we put the duke." Beauty strews the roses of her cheek, if one may say it, at his feet. A very great personage, indeed, with revenues (sometimes) that have their fountain-head in the immemorial past; the owner of half a dozen mossy villages, or perhaps a fat slice of London; a sojourner in spacious town houses and ancient castles stuffed with bric-à-brac and powdered lackeys. In his hand lie gifts and offices, and the mouth of the hungry placeman waters at sight of him; the hat of the poor curate out of situation lifts itself instinctively. His Grace is not merely a man of the moment, but a precious mosaic of august ancestors, a personality made almost sacred by precedent. He stands next to the throne, and if he but smile on the various human strata below him, who is not touched by his condescension?

Is it not a remarkable circumstance, then, or does it not at least seem remarkable, that the Duke of Suffolk, as I shall presently show, has no friends? Yet, however incredible it may appear on the surface, the matter is simple and rational enough at bottom; for I am speaking of that last Duke of Suffolk, who in Bloody Mary's time was always getting himself into trouble, and finally lost his head — not figuratively. Strangely enough, he is still extant, though in a much altered fashion. His revenues have taken wing; his retainers are scattered; and there is not a courtier or a dependent alive who cares a farthing whether my lord smiles or frowns. Were this poor, dismantled old duke to make even an excellent jest, — a thing he never did in the course of the sixteenth century, — there is not a sycophant of his left to applaud it. In all the broad realm of England there is none so poor to do him reverence. Spacious town houses and haughty castles with defective drainage know him no more. His name may not be found in the London directory, nor does it figure in any local guide-book that I have ever seen, excepting one. His Grace dwells obscurely in a dismal little shell of a church in the Minories, alone and disregarded. From time to time, to be sure, some stray, irrepressible Yankee tourist, learning — the Lord knows how — that the duke is in town, drops in upon his solitude; but no one else, or nearly no one else. The tumultuous tide of London life surges and sweeps around him, but he is not of it.

On the 23d of February, in the year 1554, Henry Grey, Duke of Suffolk, the father of a nine days' queen and the ingenious architect of his own calamity, was led from his chamber in the Tower to a spot on Tower Hill, and promptly decapitated, as a slight testimonial of Queen Mary's appreciation of the part he had played in Northumberland's conspiracy and some collateral enterprises. Thus, like Columbus, he got another world for his recompense.

This is known of all men, or nearly all men; but not one in a thousand of those who know it is cognizant of the fact that the head of the Duke of Suffolk, in an almost perfect state of preservation, can be seen to this day in a shabby old church somewhere near the Thames, at the lower end of the city — the Church of Holy

Trinity. It may be noted here, not irrelevantly, that an interview with his Grace costs from two shillings to three and sixpence per head — your own head, I mean.

It appears that shortly after the execution of the duke — on the night following, it is said — this fragment of him was secured by some faithful servant, and taken to a neighboring religious house in the Minories, where it was carefully packed in tannin, and where it lay hidden for many and many a year. The secret of its existence was not forgotten by the few who held it, and the authenticity of the relic is generally accepted, though there are iconoclasts who believe it to be the head of Edmund de la Pole, Earl of Suffolk, who also passed by the way of Tower Hill in 1513. But the Dantesque line of the nose and the arch of the eyebrow of the skull are duplicated in the duke's portrait in the National Portrait Gallery, and would seem to settle the question.

After the cruel fires of Smithfield and Oxford were burned out, and Protestantism, with Elizabeth, had come in again, and England awoke as from a nightmare — when this blessed day had dawned, the head was brought forth from its sequestration, and became an item in the pious assets of the church in which it had found sanctuary. Just when the exhumation took place, and the circumstances attending it, are unrecorded.

It was only by chance, during a stay in London several years ago, that these details came into my possession; but they were no sooner mine than a desire seized me to look upon the countenance of a man who had died on Tower Hill nearly three hundred and fifty years before. Surely a New Englander's hunger for antiquity could not leave such a morsel as that untouched.

Breakfasting one morning with an old London acquaintance, a gentleman named Blount, I invited him to accompany me on my pilgrimage to the Minories. There was kindness in his ready acceptance; for the last thing to interest the average Londoner is that charm of historical association which makes London the Mecca of Americans. Blount is a most intelligent young fellow, though neither a bookman nor an antiquarian, and he confessed, with the characteristic candor of his island, that he had n't heard that the Duke of Suffolk was dead!

"Only in a general way, don't you know?" he added. "They polished off so many armor-plated old duffers in those days that one would have to make a business of it in order to keep the run of them."

His views concerning the geography of the

Minories were also lacking in the quality of positiveness.

"The cabby will know how to get us there," suggested Blount optimistically.

But the driver of the hansom we picked up on Piccadilly did not seem so sanguine. "The Minories — the Minories," he repeated, smiling in a constrained, amused way, as if he thought that perhaps "the Minories" might be a kind of shell-fish. He somehow reminded me of the gentleman who asked, "What *are* Pericles?" The truth is, the London season was at its height, and the man did not care for so long a course, there being more shillings in the briefer trips.

However, as we had possession of the hansom, and as possession is nine points of the law, we directed him to take us to St. Paul's Churchyard, where we purposed to make further inquiries.

Our inquiries were destined to extend far beyond that limit, for there seemed to be a dearth of exact information as to where the Church of Holy Trinity was located. Yet the church, rebuilt in 1706, covers the site of a once famous convent, founded in 1293 by Blanche, Queen of Navarre, for the sisterhood of "Poor Clares." The convent of the Minoresses gave its name to a district which, according to Stow the historiographer, was formerly occupied by "divers fair and large storehouses for armour and habiliments of war, with divers workhouses to the same purpose." Mr. Pepys, in his diary, has frequent references to the Minories, and often went there on business. On March 24, 1663, he writes: "Thence Sir J. Minnes and I homewards, calling at Browne's the mathematician in the Minnerys, with a design of buying White's ruler to measure wood with, but could not agree on the price. So home, and to dinner." Dear old Pepys! he always makes a picture of himself. One can almost see him in the stuffy little shop, haggling with Browne over the price of White's ruler. It is still a street for shops in Browne's line of trade. Here, above the door of John Owen, dealer in nautical and astronomical instruments, may be observed the wooden image of the Little Midshipman, introduced to all the world by Mr. Dickens in the pages of "Dombey and Son"—the Little Midshipman, with one leg still thrust forward, and the preposterous sextant at his eye, taking careful observations of nothing.

But to return to the church. Singularly enough, the ground upon which it stands is a portion of the handsome estate granted by Edward VI to the Duke of Suffolk in smoother days. So, when all is said, there seems a sort of poetic fitness in his occupancy of the place. I wish it had been of easier access.

I do not intend to enumerate the difficulties we encountered in discovering the Duke's claustral abode. To mention half of them would be to give to my slight structure of narrative a portico vastly larger than the edifice itself.

After a tedious drive through a labyrinth of squalid streets and alleys — after much filling and backing and a seemingly fruitless expenditure of horse — we finally found ourselves knocking at a heavily clamped door of wrinkled oak, obviously belonging to an ancient building, though it looked no older than the surrounding despondent brickwork. There was a bit of south wall, however, not built within the memory or record of man.

The door presently swung back on its rheumatic hinges, and we were admitted into the vestibule by a man who made no question of our right to enter — the verger, apparently: a middle-aged person, slender and pallid, as if he were accustomed to dwell much in damp subterranean places. He had the fragile, waxen look of some vegetable that has eccentrically sprouted in a cellar. It was no strain on the imagination to fancy that he had been born in the crypt. Making a furtive motion of one hand to his forehead by way of salute, the man threw open a second door, and ushered us into the church, a high arched space filled with gloom that appeared to have soured and turned into a stale odor. The heavy balks of time-stained oak that supported the roof were half lost in the dimness overhead. The London idea of daylight drifted in through several tall, narrow windows of smoky glass set in lead, and blended genially with the pervading dust.

The church was scarcely larger than an ordinary chapel, and contained nothing of note. There were some poor monuments to the Dartmouth family, and here and there a hideous mural tablet to nobody in particular. The woodwork was black with age, and not noticeable for its carving. A registry kept here of those who died in the parish during the plague of 1665 scarcely stimulated curiosity; nor could the imagination be widely dilated by the circumstance that the body of Sir Philip Sidney once lay in state in the chancel, while preparations were making in St. Paul's for national obsequies to the hero of Zutphen. The *pièce de résistance* — indeed, the sole dish of the banquet — was clearly that head which, three centuries and more ago, had had so little discretion as to get itself chopped off. I was beginning to query if the whole thing were not a fable, when Blount, with an assumed air of sprightly interest, demanded to see the relic.

"Certingly, sir," said the man, stroking a fungus growth of grayish side-whiskers. "I wishes there was more gentlemen in your way of thinking; but 'ardly nobody cares for it now-adays, and it is a *most* hinteresting hobject. If it was in the British Museum, sir, there'd be no hend of ladies and gentlemen flocking to look at it. But this is n't the British Museum, sir."

It was not; but the twilight, and the silence, and the loneliness of the place made it the more proper environment.

"You must have some visitors, however," I suggested.

"Mostly Hamericans, sir. Larst week, sir," — and a wan light that would have been a smile on any other face glimmered through the man's pallor, — "larst week, sir, there was a gent 'ere as wanted to buy the dook."

I recognized my countryman!

"A descendant of the Greys, no doubt," I remarked brazenly.

"Begging your parding, sir, this branch of the family was hextinct in Mary Tudor's reign, or shortly hafter."

"Well," said Blount, "since you did n't sell his Grace, suppose you let us have a look at him."

Taking down a key suspended against the wall on a nail, the verger unlocked a cupboard, and drew forth from its pit-like darkness a tin box, perhaps eighteen inches in height and twelve inches square, containing the head. This he removed from the case, and carefully placed in my hands, a little to my surprise. A bodiless head, I am convinced, has dramatic qualities that somehow do not appertain in a like degree to a headless body. The dead duke in his entirety would not have caused me the same start. After an instant of wavering, I carried the relic into the light of one of the windows for closer inspection, Blount meanwhile looking over my shoulder.

"'E used to 'ave a very good 'ead of 'air," remarked the verger, "but not in my time; in my great-grandfather's, maybe."

A few spears of brittle hair — not more than five or six at most — now turned to a reddish brown, like the dried fibres of the cocoanut, still adhered to the cranium. At the base of the severed vertebra I noticed a deep indentation, showing that the executioner had faltered at first, and had been obliged to strike a second blow in order to complete his work. A thin integument, yellowed in the process of embalming, like that of a mummy, completely covered the skull, which was in no manner repulsive.

It might have been a piece of mediæval carving in dark wood, found in some chantry choir, or an amiable gargoyle from a cathedral roof.

"There's a sort of hagony in that hupper lip, don't you think, sir?"

The verger's remark was purely perfunctory, a sample of his elegiac stock in trade. Skulls have an unpleasant habit of looking sardonic or dissatisfied, and no wonder. This one retained a serene human expression such as I never saw in any other.

"No," I said. "If his Grace had fallen asleep in his armchair after a soothing dinner, his mien could not have been more placid."

As I gazed upon the sharply cut features, they suddenly seemed familiar, and I had that odd feeling, which has often come to me in cathedral towns in England, and especially during my walks through the older sections of old London — the impression of having once been a part of it all, as possibly I was in some remote period. At this instant, with my very touch upon a tangible something of that haunting Past — at this instant, I repeat, the gloomy church, and Blount, and the verger, and all of the life that is, slipped away from me, and I was standing on Tower Hill with a throng of other men-at-arms, keeping back the motley London rabble at the point of our halberds —

rude, ill-begotten knaves, that ever rejoice at the downfall of their betters.

It is a shrewish winter morning, and nipping airs creep up, unwanted, from the river; for we have been standing here these three hours, chilled to the bone, under the bend of that sullen sky. Fit weather for such work, say I. Scarcely a day but a head falls. Within the fortnight my Lord Guilford, and the Lady Jane — and she only in her fewers — and others hastening on! 'T is best not be born too near the purple. Perhaps 't were better not be born at all. What times are these! — with the king's death, and the plottings, and the burnings, and the bodies of men hanging from gibbets everywhere, in Southwark and Westminster, at Temple Bar and Charing Cross — upward of tenscore of silly fellows that had no more brains than to dabble in sedition at mad Wyatt's bidding.

What times, indeed! The carven images, with new heads on, have crept forth from their hiding; we say mass once more, and God hath come back to us in a wafer — "the baker made him," quoth poor Lady Jane! (The sweet soul was as ready with her blithe word as a wench at a fair.) Kings come and go, but Smithfield fires die not down. Now the Catholic burns, and now the heretic — and both for God's glory.

Methinks the sum of evil done on this earth through malice is small by the side of the evil done with purblind good intent. 'Twixt fool and knave, the knave is the safer man. There's no end to the foolishness of the fool, but the knave hath the limits of his intelligence. The very want of wit that stops the one keeps the other a-going. Ah, will it ever be merry world in England again, when a mortal may eat his crust and drink his pint without fear of halter or fagot? What with the cruel bishops, and the Hot Gospelers—crazy folk all!—and this threatened Spanish marriage, peace is not like to thrive. Why should English Mary be so set to wed with a black Spaniard! How got she such a bee in her bonnet to sting us all? Faith, now I think on it, she's one half Spain through Catherine of Arragon.

Hark! From somewhere in the Tower the sound of a tolling bell is blown to us across the open. At last! A gate is flung back, and through the archway advances a little group of men. The light sparkles on the breastplates and morions of the guards in front. The rest are in sad-colored clothes. In that group, methinks, are two or three that need be in no hot haste to get here! On they come, slowly, solemnly, between the double lines of steel, the spearmen and the archers. Nearer and nearer, pausing not, nor hurrying. And now they reach the spot.

How pale my lord is, holding in his hand a lemon stuck with cloves for his refreshment! And yet he wears a brave front. He does not look at me, but in days that were not heavy like this day my lord knew me right well, for I have many a time ridden behind him to the Duke of Northumberland's county seat, near Isleworth by the Thames. Perchance 't was even there, at Syon House, they spun the web that tripped them — and I not sniffing treason the while! My lord was not wise to mix himself in such dark matters. I pray he make a fair end of it, like to that angel his daughter, who, though no queen, poor soul! laid down her life in queenly fashion. These great folk, who have everything soft to make their beds of — so they throw it not away — have somehow learned to die as stoutly as any of the baser sort, who are accustomed. May it be so with my lord! . . .

He motions as if he would speak to the multitude. Listen! Yes, thank God! he will die true Protestant; and so, stand back, Sir Priest! He hath no use for thy ghostly services. Stand back! (I breathe this only to myself, else were my neck not worth a ha'penny!) Thus did she wish it in her prayers, the Lady Jane; thus did she beg him to comport himself — she, at this hour a ten days' saint in heaven. Death shall not turn him from his faith, he says — and proves it. Ah, Master Luther, what a brave seed thou hast sown in Wycliffe's furrow! . . . And now the headsman kneels to beg my lord's forgiveness. "God forgive thee, as I do," he answers gently, and no tremble in the voice! I could weep, were I not a queen's man and under-officer, and dared do it.

And now he binds a handkerchief about his eyes, and now he kneels him to the block. Once more his lips move in speech. What is it he saith? "Lord, into thy hands I commend my spirit!"—

"What you 'ear rattling, sir," observed the verger, "is a tooth that 's dropped hinside. I keeps it there for a curiosity. It seems to hadd to the hinterest."

The spell was broken.

The spell was broken, but the rigid face that confronted me there in the dim light was a face I had known in a foregone age. The bitter morning on Tower Hill, the surging multitude, the headsman with his axe — it was not a dream; it was a memory!

I silently placed the relic in the verger's hands, and turned away, whispering to Blount to fee the man.

"By Jove!" exclaimed Blount, rejoining me at the church door. Then he said thoughtfully — thoughtfully, that is, for him: "Do you suppose a fellow takes any interest in himself after he is dead, or knows what 's going on in this world?"

"There are more things in heaven and earth, Horatio Blount, than are dreamed of in our philosophy. Perhaps he does."

"Well, then, if a fellow does, that old boy can't be over and above pleased at being made a blooming peep-show of, don't you know."

I agreed with Blount. And now that so many years have gone by, — and especially as I have seen the thing myself, — it seems to me it would be a proper act for some hand gently to inurn the head of that luckless old nobleman with the rest of him, which lies, it is said, under the chancel pavement of St. Peter's, in the Tower, close by the dust of Anne Boleyn in her pitiful little elm-wood shell originally used for holding arrows. This brings me back to my starting point:

Has the Duke of Suffolk no friends?

Since these pages were written, the Church of Holy Trinity has been demolished in the march of improvement. His Grace the Duke has consequently sought a domicile elsewhere; but just where I have had no heart to inquire.

SHAW'S FOLLY

I

Many years ago an old friend of mine named Shaw made an experiment which, though it failed lamentably, has a kind of interest attaching to it as an early attempt to do in a small way what has since been successfully accomplished on a large scale. My account of the experiment referred to would doubtless have taken the shape of a sober essay on economics, were it not for certain collateral happenings which might have seemed out of place in a serious paper. As I am unwilling to suppress the lighter material, the presentation of the matter must necessarily be in a different form.

On West Fifteenth Street, and midway between two of those great arteries which stretch up from the commercial heart of the city, stands a block of brownstone English-basement houses of that monotonous style of architecture peculiar to New York. From the cornice of the flat, tin-plated roof down to the escutcheon at the keyhole of the area door, these houses are so exactly alike that it has chanced to more than one occupant, returning home late at night, to try his pass-key on the wrong domicile. I imagine that families residing here might gradually come to resemble one another morally and physically, until at last it would make very little difference which front door they used. This would be the natural result, if the said families did not occasionally pile their household belongings into huge vans, and move themselves to another row of buildings of the same enervating uniformity.

Such complete fusion of identities as I have hinted at as possible had certainly not taken place in this particular block at the moment the present record opens. The three persons who were seated, one May evening long ago, in the rear parlor of the centre house in the series bore slight resemblance, I fancy, to any other three persons assembled under the roofs which impartially covered the various cells of that human hive.

The individuals in question were seated near a round table, upon which stood a drop-light from the chandelier, and consisted of one man and two women. Their relations described themselves at once as those of father, mother, and daughter. The father, a person in the early autumn of life, was reading, or pretending to read, the evening newspaper. The mother, also in her sunny prime, held a piece of sewing-work in her hand; held it listlessly, letting the needle take long vacations. The daughter, a handsome girl of eighteen or nineteen, was bending over a novel, from whose pages she lifted her eyes at brief intervals, glancing in a hurried, evasive way at her two elders in turn.

There was something indefinable in the atmosphere of the richly furnished room — a constraint, an anxiety, an air of reticence and hesitation which seemed to communicate itself to the ormolu clock as it slowly and with apparent effort measured out eight strokes, holding back the eighth as if it were deliberating whether or not to tell the whole truth about the hour.

The timepiece had not ceased vibrating (with suppressed emotion, as it were) when the gentleman began to fold up the journal into a small compass, to which he gave a final twist, preparatory to laying it on the table. This he presently did. The elder of the two women let the needle-work slip into her lap, and looked at him anxiously across the newspaper, which now lay writhing and trying to untwist itself on the marble slab.

"Yes, my dear," he remarked, intercepting the interrogation that flitted across her features,

"I think I'll drop down to the club for an hour."

The words were spoken lightly, but there was somehow a false note in the lightness. The wife mechanically resumed her sewing, and remained silent. The young girl, who had raised her head quickly, again bent over the page which she had not been reading.

As the man crossed the apartment and stepped into the hall, the women glanced at each other with an enigmatical expression on their faces; but neither of them spoke or moved. The clock, breathing heavily on its black walnut bracket, seemed the only thing alive in the room, until the street door was heard to close, when the young girl immediately left her seat, and passing swiftly to a window in the front parlor, lifted one corner of the gray holland shade. As she did it, her face showed anxiously in the flare of the street lamp opposite the house.

"Which way has he gone?" asked the elder woman. She had risen, and was standing beside the rocking-chair.

"Toward Sixth Avenue."

"Are you sure?"

"Yes, mother."

"And the club is in the other direction?"

The girl nodded her head.

"I can't bear it," said the woman; "I had no sleep last night. I cannot stand it any longer."

"You mean to follow him, mother?"

"I mean to know what is going on. It is useless for you to argue with me, Elizabeth. I intend to follow him."

The words were spoken in a manner which showed that some action of this sort had previously been opposed by the daughter. The daughter offered no opposition now, but with her lips tightly compressed left the room. She shortly reappeared, bringing some wraps thrown over one arm. A moment afterward the two women descended the brown-stone steps of the house, and paused an instant on the sidewalk.

II

When Augustus Shaw retired from business he was forty-five years old. His withdrawal from the firm of Shaw, Woods and Company was a surprise to the world—that is to say, to such fraction of the world as had had commercial intercourse with him. It was more than a surprise to his father, Elijah Shaw, a remarkably well-preserved old gentleman of eighty, who had not ceased to look upon his son as an immature youth still requiring the oversight of the paternal eye. Shaw senior, who resided in

Vermont, was at the time visiting a married daughter in the city.

"I don't approve of it," said the old gentleman. "Augustus has thrown up a business that was coining money like a mint; and that's not the worst of it. What will become of the boy, with nothing to do from morning till night? He 'll be sure to tumble into some sort of foolishness. It 's very dangerous at his age to have no regular employment. A country life is the only thing for Augustus now. He ought to buy some of those neglected lands up in New Hampshire, and become an abandoned farmer. A big city full of pitfalls like New York is no place for him. It 's no place for anybody. If a man 's poor, he can't live here; and if he 's rich, he 'd better not."

Augustus's view of the case was this: For twenty years and upward he had been a slave to business, a supremely successful slave as it happened, and he had extracted a certain kind of satisfaction from success merely as success; but the process had tied him down and involved many self-denials. He was now in the prime of life, with a fortune far beyond the dream of the sixteen-year-old Vermont boy, who had walked into New York with twenty dollars in his pocket and the determination suffused throughout him to be a rich man some day.

Why should he continue to heap up money until he was a spavined old fellow incapable of getting any comfort out of his accumulations? What was the use of wealth to a man who was obliged to soak his toast in tea and could not ride in his carriage without taking his rheumatism along with him? A good dinner is a mockery when you have no digestion left. He purposed to dine before such calamity should befall him, and to drive out unaccompanied by anything less agreeable than Maria.

Indeed, his plans were in a special manner designed with reference to Mrs. Shaw. During the acquirement of his fortune his home life had been a mere episode; he had never leisurely warmed his hands at his own fireside. He was to open a new account with life. He would take Maria and his daughter to theatres and concerts and picture exhibitions, as he had seldom been able to do when his evenings were his only hours of rest. He would make visits, and give little dinners, and read what 's-his-name's novels, and see something of the social world. The supervision of his investments would give him as much occupation as he desired to have in a business way.

"Augustus has made a mistake," persisted old Mr. Shaw, "and he 'll discover it when it 's too late. Before twelve months are over he 'll assemble and vote himself a fool, mark my prediction, Maria" — for it was to that lady these reassuring words were addressed after having vainly been placed at the disposal of Augustus.

The younger Mr. Shaw's dream of domesticity did not come true at once, nor, indeed, did it ever materialize precisely as he had expected. In settling his relations with the firm a hundred points arose, each entailing some vexatious delay; but finally matters were adjusted, and Augustus Shaw became one of those *rarae aves* in our busy American life — a gentleman of leisure.

Immediately on his retirement Mr. Shaw and the family moved to their cottage at Long Branch. The summer passed pleasantly; but Mr. Shaw had never before had so much seaside at one time, and as the season drew to a close he became impatient to get back to the city. The family left Long Branch somewhat in advance of the general exodus, and the first week in September saw them again established in West Fifteenth Street.

After the bloom of novelty was brushed off, Mr. Shaw found that amusement as a permanent occupation was far from being a simple matter. In order to achieve even a moderate success in it, it is indispensable that one should have a long line of ancestors austerely trained in the art of doing nothing. Augustus Shaw could not comply with this requisition. He had come of plain New England people, who believed in the gospel of toil, and had practiced it to the end, some on the land and some on the sea. There had been rich Shaws before his time, — ship-captains, and farmers, and lawyers, — and they had nearly always made a bee-line from the quarter-deck, the plow, or the judicial bench to the family burial-ground. He was the first of his race to withdraw from active life without the special intervention of Providence.

The Shaw family had few acquaintances and no intimates that were not in a manner dependents. Mr. Shaw was a wealthy man for those days, — the days just preceding the period when millionaires were to become monotonous, — and with a little social tact the Shaw family could easily have made their way. But social tact is an inborn faculty, and the Shaws were without it. On the edge of the great world they continued to live simply and quietly, and, perhaps with the exception of Mr. Shaw, not unhappily. He was the only one of the three lacking internal resources. Mrs. Shaw's heart was in her housekeeping, and Elizabeth led a busy and variegated existence in the realms of fiction.

Mr. Shaw was no great reader outside of newspapers. Politics interested him deeply; but he had no personal aspirations politically, and remained a spectator. When he cut himself adrift from his counting-room he was stranded. It is not to be deduced from all this that Mr. Augustus Shaw was a nonentity. He was a man of unusually keen perceptions and great executive capacity in certain lines. A lapse of judgment had thrown him out of his proper groove.

The Shaws now gave little dinners, according to the programme, and went much to the theatre — too much for Mr. Shaw, who seldom cared for the play, and would vastly have preferred his evening journal and that ten minutes' after-dinner nap which long years of nightly fatigue had crystallized into a custom. But this was a thing of the past; for even on off nights — the nights of no theatre — the evening journal failed to soothe the restlessness he had generated during the day.

At first he went down town in the forenoons; but a man of leisure in Wall Street is a solecism. Mr. Shaw speedily gave up his visits to the Merchants' Exchange and the contiguous musty offices where his presence once had some meaning; and then the heaviness of the forenoon differed in no respect from the heaviness of the afternoon. Mr. Shaw had got himself elected one of the vice-presidents of a benevolent society. The days when there was a directors' meeting were red-letter days to him. In a word, he was dreadfully bored.

Mrs. Shaw was struck by the surface changes that had taken place in her husband, and presently detected the cause. Home life was plainly insufficient for a man like Augustus, who had been used to managing large enterprises, and he must have outside interests to distract his mind. For one thing, he must have his club to go to — not a literary or an artistic club, nor a mere lunching-place, like the place down town, but an all-round club, with a predominant sprinkling of bankers, lawyers, and men of affairs generally. Such an organization was not difficult to find, and nothing was easier than to obtain membership. Mr. Woods, Mr. Shaw's late partner, arranged it with his own club, into which in due time Mr. Shaw was handsomely received.

"Maria never had a better idea," said Augustus, discussing the subject later with his father, whose mind was somewhat disturbed by certain aspects of the case. "Of course, governor, there is card-playing, for those who like it, and the members have their something-and-soda; but all in a rational way, you understand. Oh, no wilderness at all. Quiet, comfortable rooms, with easy-chairs, and newspapers, and good company. I am very glad to meet a lot of my old business acquaintances again."

"Well, Augustus, I hope it is all for the best. What 's the use!"

"Maria," observed Mr. Shaw, after Shaw senior had taken his departure, "father is a dear old boy, and the soul of honesty. I owe him everything. If it had n't been for him I should probably have been somebody else, and then I might n't have married you. Yes, father is a dear old boy; but when he runs down from Vermont for a few weeks' visit to Sodom and Gomorrah, as he calls New York and Brooklyn, I am glad that he stays at my sister's."

The success of Mrs. Shaw's expedient met her desires. The cloud was lifted from the evening fireside. Augustus had somewhere to go. Occasionally he would drop into the club of an afternoon to look over the papers, and twice a week he joined a sedate whist party there. Ultimately, the drama and the opera having more or less palled on the entire family, Mr. Shaw fell into the habit of passing an hour at the club after dinner whenever nothing else intervened. Just as the clock chimed eight he would fold up his journal, smile pleasantly on Maria and Elizabeth, and depart from the Shaw mansion, leaving the two women wholly contented, one with her hem and the other with her book or magazine. Sometimes the Delaney girls of Waverly Place, or young Simson from over the way — he was suspected of sentiment in connection with Elizabeth — would look in on them. Life flowed smoothly and sunnily with the Shaw family.

But nothing lasts in this mutable world. There is always a little rift ready to develop itself in anybody's lute. One night Elizabeth had a slight faint turn, which alarmed her mother unnecessarily, and Mr. Shaw was sent for. He was not to be found at the club, and the messenger on inquiring at what hour Mr. Shaw had left was informed by the hall-boy that the gentleman had not been in the club-house since Monday afternoon — it was then Friday. This singular statement distracted Mrs. Shaw's attention for an instant from Elizabeth's faintness, which, moreover, had passed. Of course the hall-boy was mistaken, the stupid hall-boy! Two minutes later, when Augustus returned — seeming to show that he must have started for home just before the messenger reached the club — the matter had faded out of Mrs. Shaw's mind in her relief at Elizabeth's recovery. It did not occur to her until three or four days afterward, as she was sitting alone in the back parlor.

It was one of Mr. Shaw's whist evenings, and Elizabeth had gone to the theatre with the Delaney girls. Mrs. Shaw's needle came to a dead stop in the hem as the recollection of the hall-boy's statement suddenly drifted into her thought. She ought to have told Augustus about it at the time. She would tell him the moment he came in. How odd of her to have forgotten the circumstance, and with what persistency it seemed to obtrude itself upon her now! All the details of the trivial incident grew curiously vivid. She recalled the expressionless face of James, the indoor man, and the very intonation of his voice, as he said, "The hall-boy says, ma'am, as Mr. Shaw has n't been in the club-house since last Monday."

It was eleven o'clock when Elizabeth returned, and Mr. Shaw had not appeared. He never remained out so late. Something unusual must have happened. Visions of apoplexy and garroters flitted through Mrs. Shaw's imagination. The papers at the time were full of accounts of night assaults on belated pedestrians. It had become fashionable, in a way, to be garroted. Elizabeth had been taken to and from the theatre in the coupé, and Dennis was on the point of turning to drive off to the stable when he received an order to call at the club for Mr. Shaw.

"You need n't sit up, Elizabeth," said her mother, lowering the gas in the hall. "I'll wait for your father. You look tired."

Having sent the servants to bed, Mrs. Shaw seated herself at the parlor window, where the half-drawn shade gave her a view of the deserted street, and watched for the carriage. After what seemed an interminable lapse of time the coupé came back — empty. Mr. Shaw was not in the club-house, and had not been there that night!

"That's all, Dennis," Mrs. Shaw managed to say; "the servants don't appear to know Mr. Shaw by sight."

Then she closed the street door, to which she had hastened, and sat down in a chair near the hat-rack. Her first fear for the safety of Augustus had vanished. The idea of apoplexy or garroters would have been welcome if it could have dispelled the unformed apprehensions that now possessed her. Augustus had not gone to the club that night, and he had not gone there the night Elizabeth was taken ill! The hall-boy's report had been correct — it was a part of his duty to take note of the coming and going of members. Augustus was deceiving her in some way. He had got into some dreadful trouble. His mysterious conduct was inexplicable on any other grounds. These secret movements could mean nothing else. Old Elijah Shaw, at whom they all had laughed, had been right in his dismal forebodings. But in what shape had they come true? A hundred fancies started up in her mind, like spectres indistinct and conjectural. Mrs. Shaw was not naturally a jealous woman; to be sure she had never been tested; but jealousy is a trait that betrays itself without provocation, it crops out in countless illogical directions. She had never given the faintest sign of it, but at this moment Mrs. Shaw, like Othello, was "perplexed in the extreme," and a strange spasm contracted her heart as she sat there in the dimly lighted hall.

Elizabeth must be told; indeed, the matter could not be kept from her. Hastily shutting off the gas on the lower floor, Mrs. Shaw groped her way up to Elizabeth's room, and a few minutes afterward the two repaired to Mrs. Shaw's apartment, where they engaged in disjointed conversation while the elder woman was undressing. Elizabeth had come back from Wallack's sleepy and fatigued, but now her expression was animated and her eyes in the subdued light of the chamber had the bloom of sapphires. The girl's excitement, however, was very much less than her mother's. The odd impression that all this was like something in a novel blended itself with the reality of Elizabeth's trouble, and probably modified it. Her relative composure under the circumstances piqued her mother.

"You will at least admit, Elizabeth," said Mrs. Shaw, tossing her rings into a small jewel-box on the toilet table, "that your father is acting very strangely."

"Yes, mother; I don't understand it."

"He pretends to go to the club every night, and never goes there, it seems. Where, then, *does* he go?"

"Why don't you ask him, mother, when he comes home? I should, if I were you."

"Would you?"

"Yes, mother."

"As he is clearly trying to keep it from us, that would simply put him on his guard."

"But suppose he is n't guarding anything? It is so unlike papa."

"You are talking nonsense, Elizabeth. He *is* guarding something. Do you think it likely he'd tell us what, if we questioned him, since he's doing all he can to hide it? He does n't like to be questioned, even at the best of times. It's one of his ways. He seems to be cultivating some new ones that I have n't got used to. 'So unlike papa!' — Elizabeth, anything is like any man. No, I shall say nothing to your father," continued Mrs. Shaw, whose lips had grown thin and white. "I shall wait, and find out for myself what it all means. I don't intend to be put off with prevarications and half-truths. I intend to discover everything."

"But how will you discover — everything, mother?" said the girl, with a perceptible thrill.

"You can help me, Elizabeth, if you choose. If you don't, I shall do it alone."

"Do what?"

"To-morrow night when he goes to his club" — and Mrs. Shaw lingered on the words with a wan, ironical smile — "I shall follow him."

"Oh, don't do that, mother!" cried Elizabeth. "If what seems so mysterious should turn out to be something easily explained, papa would never forgive you. Dear papa! he has never been so nice to us as he has been these last three or four months."

"That 's a very unfavorable symptom," replied Mrs. Shaw, with a worldly cynicism so foreign to her that Elizabeth gave a little start.

At that instant the click of a pass-key was heard in the lock at the street door. Elizabeth gathered her pretty night-wraps about her and fled. Mrs. Shaw reduced the dressing-table gas-jet to a mere speck, and was almost instantly sound asleep.

After an appreciable interval the staircase

began to creak, in the ingenious and malicious fashion of staircases after midnight. On the second landing somebody appeared to have run against something, presumably a three-footed stand with a pot plant on it, and a repressed remark was faintly audible. Then Mr. Shaw, carrying a shoe in each hand, passed noiselessly into the conjugal chamber. He at once extinguished the gas, and proceeded to lay aside his habiliments with that scrupulous care to avoid disturbing anybody which characterizes the man weakly conscious of having stayed out too late. Nevertheless, one or two mischances occurred: a coat was carefully laid over the back of a chair that was not there, and, later, a silver half-dollar slipped from his trousers pocket and rolled along a strip of inlaid flooring not covered by the Turkish rug. It seemed as if the coin was never going to stop rolling. Finally it slapped itself down and then indulged in a series of spasmodic efforts to get up on its rim again. But even that did not awaken Mrs. Shaw.

The breakfast next morning was a gloomy ceremony attended by two female headaches and one male conscience ill at ease. On the completion of the meal, Mr. Shaw disappeared, probably went down town, and was not seen again until half an hour before dinner. The dinner consisted of the breakfast gloom served in five courses. Mr. Shaw made several overtures to be gay, but meeting no encouragement, fell silent. Mrs. Shaw still showed traces of the previous night's agitation, and Elizabeth's theatre headache still lingered. Dinner over, Mrs. Shaw automatically picked up her needlework, Elizabeth began a new chapter in "Lady Audley's Secret," and Mr. Shaw ostentatiously unfolded the evening newspaper.

Thus were the three members of the Shaw family occupied at the moment of our first sight of them, and then ensued that brief scene, already rehearsed, in which Mr. Shaw was represented as setting forth for his club, followed rather dramatically by his wife and his daughter Elizabeth.

III

The two women paused an instant at the foot of the steps, then walked rapidly down the street toward Sixth Avenue. West Fifteenth Street was not then a crowded thoroughfare even by day, and after nightfall the passing was infrequent. Mrs. Shaw and Elizabeth met no one until they were within fifty paces of the avenue, when the elder woman grasped the girl's wrist, and they both halted abruptly. Near the corner was a small confectionery shop, from the door of which Mr. Shaw was leisurely emerging. In his hand he held a white paper parcel tied with ribbon. The shaft of light falling upon him from the shop window revealed this detail. He walked to the curbstone of the crossing on the avenue and stopped. The constant stream of pedestrians flowing in two opposite directions hid him for a moment from the mother and daughter. Though he had had the advantage of only a three minutes' start, they would have missed him if he had not stepped into the shop to make a purchase.

"He is waiting for a car," said Elizabeth, in a low voice; "an uptown or a downtown car. I wonder which?"

"It does n't matter," answered Mrs. Shaw; "if he takes either we may as well go home. You don't see a cab anywhere, Elizabeth?"

There was no cab in sight, and the nearest carriage-stand was several blocks away. The jingling bell of an approaching horse-car was now heard. It passed on unhailed, and Mr. Shaw was seen crossing the track to the opposite curb, on reaching which he turned to the left and proceeded down the avenue.

The side of the street he had selected was comparatively deserted, there being few or no shops, and Mrs. Shaw and Elizabeth, hidden by the throng on the parallel sidewalk, could observe unperceived all Mr. Shaw's movements. There was nothing mysterious about them, so far. He walked with the air of a man who had a predetermined destination, but was in no special haste to reach it. Of the three, Elizabeth and her mother were the more likely to invite notice. They were unused to being on the streets alone at night, and the novelty of it, together with the nature of their purpose, gave to them a faltering, half-terrified manner calculated to attract attention. A policeman on a corner stared them out of countenance, and wheeling partly round watched the receding figures until he lost them in the crowd.

Indeed, other eyes than those of policemen took casual note of the pair. Their costume and gait differentiated them from the frequenters of the Sixth Avenue, for almost every avenue in the great city has its own type; and then Elizabeth's beauty was not of a kind to pass unchallenged anywhere. Twice she was aware that some one turned and followed them for half a block or so; and once she was ready to drop when a beggar woman lightly touched her on the shoulder.

The sidewalks lay in a glare like that of noonday. Drug-stores, with gaudy purple and orange jars, and drinking-saloons, with knots of hard-featured men lounging at the stained-glass doorways, took turns in accentuating the fatal commonness of the street. The two women passed these latter places shrinkingly. Years afterwards, when Miss Shaw was Mrs. Rush Simson, she could not relate the story of that night expedition without throwing a little shiver into the narrative.

Meanwhile Mr. Shaw tranquilly continued his promenade, which threatened to last forever. He had gone perhaps five or six blocks, when he turned to the right into a cross-street. Proceeding a short distance down this, he again turned to the right, and entered a narrower and less well-lighted thoroughfare. Here his pace slackened. It was evident that he had nearly reached the desired point. A few steps farther on he stopped. Mrs. Shaw and Elizabeth, who had not lost sight of him for a second, were within a dozen yards of the spot where he halted. Had Mr. Shaw suspected their presence, he would not have been able to distinguish the two trembling figures blotted out by the black shadow thrown from the high board fence inclosing some vacant lots just opposite. Mr. Shaw himself, standing in a square of light, was distinctly visible.

The street was of seedy aspect — one of those streets which seem to have started out in life with some pretensions to gentility, but have been unfortunate, and become despondent, and have finally relinquished the struggle.

Here and there the old-fashioned moulding of a doorway indicated that the grimy red-brick house to which it belonged had once known happier days, perhaps as the residence of some prosperous Pearl Street merchant in the early forties, who was laughed at for erecting a mansion so far uptown.

It was in front of such a building, though it had recently been painted and otherwise smartened up, that Mr. Shaw halted — a tall building four windows wide, with heavily carved stone lintels. The basement was occupied by a grocery store brilliantly lighted. On each of the three succeeding floors the closely-drawn yellow shades were also illuminated — evidently a well-filled tenement house of the better class. At the left of the shop a steep flight of stone steps, with iron railings of a bygone pattern, led up to a double door, a wing of which was open. Mr. Shaw mounted these steps and passed into the dusky vestibule without hesitation, like one to whom the topography of the place was perfectly familiar.

Elizabeth and her mother, who had not exchanged a word since they quitted the avenue, stood huddled together, gazing with wonderment at the façade of the house into which Mr. Shaw had disappeared so unexpectedly. Oblivious of everything but the fact that he had crossed the threshold of this strange house as if it had been the threshold of his own home, they crouched there in the dark, holding their breath, dumb and motionless, like a group of statuary. Over the way a drunken man reeled by singing "When Johnnie Comes Marching Home"; but they neither saw nor heard him.

Possibly five minutes had elapsed when Mrs. Shaw suddenly loosened her hand from Elizabeth's and pointed to a window — a window in the second story. A sharp silhouette of Mr. Shaw's head and bust had fixed itself against the yellow shade. The grotesque shadow was so lifelike that it might have spoken. The slight tuft of hair standing up from the forehead would have made Elizabeth smile if the circumstances had been less sinister and bewildering.

"What can Augustus be doing there?" whispered Mrs. Shaw, finding her voice.

"I cannot imagine, mother," Elizabeth whispered back. "That certainly is papa."

"Unless there are two of him. Why is he in that room? Look, Elizabeth! — he seems to be laughing at something."

The lips of the profile were parted for an instant, but no sound issued from them audible to the outsiders. That laugh was all the more uncanny and phantomish for being unheard.

"What *does* it mean!" exclaimed Mrs. Shaw.

As she spoke, a second shape joined the first — the silhouette of a woman wearing some sort of cap and holding a child, which she tossed up several times, and then placed in the arms of the other shadow, and then the whole picture vanished like a flash, leaving the bright square of yellow cloth a blank.

The little drama had not lasted sixty seconds. The two spectators in the street below still stood with uplifted faces, incredulous of their own eyes.

"Oh, tell me that we dreamt it, mother!" cried Elizabeth. "Tell me that we're asleep in our beds at home, and this is only a nightmare, the beginning of some horrible dream!"

"I am afraid it is the ending of a happy one, Elizabeth," answered her mother, who had grown strangely calm within the minute. "Let us go back. We will take a car on the avenue. Come!"

IV

When Mr. Shaw returned home that night, Elizabeth, half disrobed, was walking aimlessly about her bedroom; but Mrs. Shaw was seated as usual near the round table in the rear parlor. From its mural bracket the little clock, which appears to perform the rôle of Greek chorus in this recital, announced the hour of ten, as Mr. Shaw entered the apartment. Mrs. Shaw was seated stiffly, and her face, turned three quarters away from the light, remained in shadow. She was very composed and very pale. Her pallor apparently did not escape Mr. Shaw.

"Is n't your headache any better, my dear?" he asked, reaching out to take a chair.

She did not reply for several seconds; then she lifted her face, and said: "Augustus, have you brought home the confectionery?"

Mr. Shaw started, and flushed a faint crimson. "The confectionery!" he repeated.

"Augustus," said his wife, rising from the chair, a trifle paler, but retaining her curious self-possession, "I know everything."

"If you know everything, then there is nothing more to be said."

"There is much more to be said. You made believe that you spent your evenings at the club. I followed you to-night."

"You followed me!"

"I followed you to the tenement house, and saw you holding the child in your arms, the child for whom you bought the candy—if it was not for the mother."

"The mother!—the candy!—why, Maria"—

"Mr. Shaw, I did n't know until now that I

had married an echo. I did n't know," added the woman wearily, "*what* I had married."

"Maria," said Mr. Shaw, recovering himself, "if I 'm behaving like an idiotic echo it 's because you upset me with your suddenness."

"My suddenness?"

"Now *you* are doing it. Suppose you don't get excited. There 's no need for it. I am sorry about this."

Silence.

"I 'm very sorry. You 've managed to frustrate a little plan of mine. I meant to give you a surprise, Maria."

"You succeeded!"

"No, I 've made a muddle of it — with your assistance. You have spoiled everything. I did n't understand at first what you were driving at; but now I see. You think I have gone wrong in some way. Well, I have n't gone very far this time; but I won't answer for the future. Do you know what is carved on the slab let into the wall over the front door of that tenement house?"

"I don't want to know."

"But you must know. The inscription on that stone cost me two shillings a letter, and the words are — THE MARIA HOME."

Mrs. Shaw gave a start in her turn.

"It 's a model tenement house for poor people,

and the plan and purpose of it are among the few things in my life that I'm not ashamed of. I'd an idea of trying to do a little good before I died. There's no money in the thing; but I wanted you to own it, and I gave your name to it, and I intended to give you the deed of the property to-morrow morning for your wedding-anniversary present."

"Augustus . . ."

"I did n't mean you to suspect a thing about it until then. I can't conceive how you came to. Maybe my staying out so late last night set your wits to work. It was after eleven, was n't it? I had a hundred and one small odds and ends to finish up. I stayed longer than I ought to have done; but they make a great deal of me down there, the children and all, and I have to step in and say a word to each of the tenants, or there'd be trouble. To-night I paid my wind-up visit as proprietor to The Maria Home. I did n't dream that the new proprietor was around."

Mrs. Shaw made a movement as if to speak, but restrained herself, and stood silent, with one hand on the back of the chair from which she had risen.

"Since I got out of business," continued Mr. Shaw, "nothing has interested me like the fixing up of that tenement house. I have been two months doing it. I've spent whole days watching the workmen. I was in such a hurry to get the place in running order that I hired the carpenters and painters to do inside work evenings. The nights I went there to superintend the job I made believe I was at the club. I had to do it, or show my hand. You will have to tell me how you discovered that I was n't at the club. And you thought I had gone dead wrong?"

"We thought something had gone wrong, Augustus. What else could we think when we found out that you were deceiving us?"

"And you actually followed me, both of you?"

"Yes, Augustus," faltered Mrs. Shaw, — "Elizabeth and I."

"Perhaps you were too old not to know any better; but I am ashamed of Elizabeth."

"Don't, Augustus! don't laugh at me, and don't blame Elizabeth. She begged me to speak to you the moment I suspected — I hardly know what. I did n't mind a word she said; and, oh, I am so sorry! Elizabeth was the only one that had a grain of reason. But even she, when we stood in that horrid street and saw you — saw you" — and the figures on that yellow window-shade flashed before Mrs. Shaw's vision.

"And you were jealous of me, were you?"

Mrs. Shaw nodded her head, but nodded it only slightly, not wanting to spill any tears.

"Madly jealous, Maria? You may as well say it."

"Yes — madly."

"Maria, what was the name of that fellow in the play the other night — that colored fellow that did n't have sense enough for an end-man in a negro-minstrel show?"

"Othello," said Mrs. Shaw, with a half-hysterical laugh.

"Well, my dear, if I were to write a play I should call it *Mrs. Othello.*"

"You are not *very* angry with me?"

"No, I am not angry at all. I'm a little mortified, I confess, and a good deal amused. Perhaps on my side I made a mistake in trying to keep anything away from you. It was n't a very wise piece of business. A man should n't hide things from his wife, nor she from him. If I ever *do* go wrong, Maria, I shall let you know in advance; I'll drop you a telegram. Where's Elizabeth? She has n't gone to bed yet, for I saw a light in her room as I came along. I wish you'd run upstairs and tell her that she has n't kissed anybody good-night."

But Mrs. Shaw, who had meanwhile sunk

into her chair, rested one arm on the edge of the table, and laid her cheek on the arm, and did not move.

V

Late that night, just as Elizabeth had drifted into a doze through sheer weariness of waiting, she was dimly conscious of some one standing outside her bedroom door. Faint as was the impression, it awakened her, and she distinctly caught the rustle of skirts and the light sound of receding footfalls. It was her mother, who had come to tell her what had taken place. Elizabeth hurriedly opened the door, and looked out into the black hallway; but by this time Mrs. Shaw had gained her own apartment, and the girl did not dare follow her.

The next morning as she descended the stairs Elizabeth's eyes were troubled and her face was nearly colorless; but at the threshold of the breakfast-room, where she had paused, the blood suddenly came into the pale cheeks and the anxious expression vanished. She stood brightening, with a motionless hand on the half-turned knob. Her father and mother were chatting gayly over the breakfast! Then Elizabeth flung back the door, and entered the room with a joyous laugh, not waiting for any explanation to lighten her heart. . . .

The three lingered long at table that morning, and when the happy conference came to an end, Elizabeth could hardly wait for the hour appointed for Dennis to drive them together to the shabby street with its mysterious house, which had been so wrapped in blackness overnight and now stood in a flood of sunshine.

"Why, it's like a story in a magazine!" cried Elizabeth. "A silhouette of papa, with that dear tuft of hair standing up straight against the window-shade, would make a delightful illustration."

"Elizabeth!" remonstrated Mrs. Shaw.

"It did n't seem so diverting last night, mother, but now, as I think of it"—and the girl broke into a laugh, in which her father joined; but Mrs. Shaw, like a dutiful wife, was never inclined to regard Augustus in a humorous light.

Thus the oddly composed cloud which had gathered over the roof of The Maria Home floated away. But it was the precursor of other clouds which, though less portentous, were not so easily dissipated. It seems an unfair dispensation of destiny that an amiable, middle-aged gentleman engaged in a work of benevolence should have as many tribulations befall him as if he had been pursuing evil courses.

Mr. Shaw's idea of establishing a model tenement house sprang from a purely philanthropic impulse. As vice-president of the benevolent society, referred to elsewhere, he had come to an intimate knowledge of how the poor were housed in a great city. His official work on committees had opened up to him vistas of wretchedness until then not dreamed of. The miserable folk of the slums, so degraded as to be unaware of their own misery, moved his pity; but this was not the class that interested him the most deeply. It was the class one or two removes above, — the men and women who would like to live cleanly lives in cleanly homes, but whose poverty condemned them to haunts of filth and darkness. Sorrow's crown of sorrow is not, as the poet says, the remembering of happier things, but the bitter consciousness of never having known them.

In vast congeries of human beings light and air, which seem the common inheritance of man, have their price, like coal and bread, and the very poor may purchase them but sparingly. To effect a radical change in this matter, or indeed, in any appreciable degree to alter the general condition of the great masses, struck Mr. Shaw as a task for dreamers. One might nibble at the edge of such an endeavor, but that was all. Still one might nibble, and turning the problem over in his mind he resolved that somewhere in the great, distracted city there should be a little nook where light and air, for a few at least, could be had at panic prices.

His plan was to construct a moderate-sized apartment house, very plain in its inside and outside finish, but embracing every device of ventilation and sanitary plumbing that money could compass. There should be a bath-room to each suite, and an elevator, and separate front-door bells, and conveniences in the way of closets hitherto unthought of in the economy of tenement houses. The apartments were to be let to worthy and respectable families at a rental just sufficient to keep the premises in repair. The interest on the investment and the taxes on the property were to be items in Mr. Shaw's personal contribution; and he would call the tenement The Maria Home, in order that a good woman's name might bring good luck to it. Mr. Shaw had always signalized the anniversary of their marriage by a gift to his wife. This year it should be something better than a jewel from Tiffany's.

A brief search resulted in his finding a building adapted to his purpose, and he at once set to work on the necessary renovations. Mr. Shaw did not overstate the case when he told his wife that nothing had so absorbed him since he retired from business; it was the one thing that had absorbed him. This tenement house was his yacht, his race-horse, his private salmon-stream. The money which other men spent on pleasures that had no attraction for him, he spent on this.

When The Maria Home was ready for occupants, Mr. Shaw issued a series of judiciously worded advertisements in daily journals read by working people, stating at what hour applications for rooms could be made on the premises. He set aside two nights in the week on which to confer with his prospective tenants, who were necessarily not at liberty during the day. The most explicit and unquestionable references were required of them, for Mr. Shaw had no intention that undeserving persons should reap the benefits appertaining to inmates of The Maria Home. One of these benefits was in connection with the grocery store already established in the basement. The proprietor was a German named Swartz, a feature of whose contract was to furnish the tenants with certain necessities, like flour, tea, and sugar, at a trifle above actual cost, Mr. Shaw making up the natural deficit thus incurred by a rebate in Swartz's rent.

The five or six suites constituting The Maria Home were not long in the market. Five families and two detached elderly females were installed before the end of a week.

The little world which Mr. Shaw had set a-going was a mixed and busy little world, the inhabitants of which were not so numerous as their occupations. To begin at the top, architecturally speaking, Mrs. Malone, in the attic, was charwoman, sick-nurse, and plain sempstress. Mrs. Ward, on the same floor, took in fine sewing, but depended chiefly on a brother in Chicago. Of the two Downey girls, the floor beneath, one was under-saleswoman in a small millinery department shop on Sixth Avenue, and the other worked in a paper-box manufactory across town; Downey, the father, did something in the old-iron and junk-bottle line. The employment of Mr. Morrison, directly over Mr. Swartz, was multifarious, and not easily to be defined — an employment that exacted eccentric hours; the son was porter in a Broadway dry-goods house, and the daughter assisted her mother. A machinist, a sign-painter, and a tailor, with their respective fledglings, completed the census.

There was an element of pathos in the intense interest which Mr. Shaw took in his scheme. He could not keep himself away from the place, and no longer having any valid reason for frequent visits, improvised important business interviews with Mr. Swartz. Presently Mr. Shaw's appearance came to be hailed with an enthusiasm that spread from Germany in the basement to Ireland in the sky-parlor. "It 's proud I am to see his Honor," Mrs. Malone would cry from the top of the staircase; and the children would gather about him on the landings, divining a friend, with the curious instinct children have. It was rarely that a paper of bonbons did not lie nestled in Mr. Shaw's coat pocket, where such delicacies were supposed to generate spontaneously.

This was the situation, and The Maria Home had been running nearly a month, the night Mrs. Shaw and Elizabeth made their discovery.

At the breakfast table the following morning Mr. Shaw told the story which I have given only in outline. He had not finished before the two women fell to making a thousand sympathetic plans. Mrs. Shaw would have a supervisory eye on the housekeeping; and a Christmas tree for the children, with some useful gift pendent from every twig, instantly took root and grew six feet high in Elizabeth's determination. Among her own acquaintances Mrs. Shaw would solicit work for the sewing-women. There was to be no measure to her interest in everything to do with the Home. Unconsciously to herself, perhaps, Mrs. Shaw was subtly atoning for the injustice she had done her husband.

With the passing of the title the duty of managing the property did not pass from Mr. Shaw. The duty had none of the disagreeable features of perfunctory matters. It would be mere recreation to keep the building in repair, collect the rent, and look after the general welfare of the tenants. The very limited amount they were called upon to expend for shelter would of course enable them to lay by something. He purposed later to advise them how to place their savings to the best advantage. No smallest thing escaped him. He took deep pride in the neat outside appearance of the house, setting an example to the squalid environments. The little chrome-yellow patch of canary-bird, in a cage hung at the entrance to the grocery store, seemed to him to light up the whole street; and he would have condoned many a shortcoming on the part of the third-floor tenants — the Downeys — because they kept a box of mignonette on one of the window-ledges. The chiropodist's tin sign, next door, with its ghastly parody of a foot which appeared to be trying to stamp out whatever spark of respectability lingered in the neighborhood, was a dreadful eyesore to Mr. Shaw.

"I should just like to extract that corn-doctor!" was his reflection.

VI

Up to this time Mr. Shaw's pleasure in The Maria Home had been unalloyed, leaving out Mrs. Shaw's tragic moment. The monthly rents were to be collected in advance, and those for May had been paid. But on the 1st of June, when the second month's rent fell due, affairs were not quite satisfactory. Mrs. Malone was full of explosive explanations and promises, and Mrs. Ward frankly admitted her inability to pay at present. She was a fragile little woman, and had come there ill. Mr. Shaw had taken her in because of her gentle manners and the something sad about her. The Downeys could produce two thirds of the required sum, and no more. Two other families begged an extension until the following Saturday. Mr. Morrison, a silent man with heavy brows, and Mr. Swartz the grocer, were the only tenants who paid in full and promptly.

Meanwhile the Shaws had migrated to Long Branch — reluctantly on the part of Elizabeth and her mother, who regretted this interruption of their personal labors. Several commissions had been obtained for the needle-woman, and further orders were promised; and Elizabeth was in the midst of forming the nucleus of a small library for the inmates of the tenement. But these and other matters had to be left in abeyance.

The necessity of going to the city now and then to attend to the business of the Home was an agreeable break in the dull routine of Mr. Shaw's seashore life. The 1st of July brought him to town for a day. He had come with the hope of finding an improvement in the financial world. Mrs. Ward, who had heard from her brother, made up for the previous month; she could not, however, discharge the current term. In the case of Mrs. Malone history repeated itself. The rest of the lodgers, with the exception of the sign-painter, met their indebtedness. This was not wholly disheartening. But on the following month the Morrisons and the Swartzes were the only ones not behindhand.

Mr. Shaw's patience under these unlooked-for set-backs was not exhausted. The New England Methodism of his youth had not hardened a very soft spot in his heart for all sorts of unfortunates, whether culpable or not. "Every man has n't had my chances," he would say. His tolerance and point of view were expressed in Newton's comment on an outcast that once passed him on the street: "Excepting for God's grace, there goes John Newton."

Mr. Shaw, however, was disappointed and perplexed, and his perplexity increased as time went on. Mrs. Ward presently fell into a chronic state of not having heard from her brother in Chicago; but she was a sick woman, and could not be put out on the sidewalk. Of Mrs. Malone, whose general suavity veiled a temperament not to be trifled with, Mr. Shaw was candidly afraid; and the September forenoon when he tapped at her door and found that charming person absent for the day, he was not half sorry. On this same occasion the Downeys might as well have been in the moon as in The Maria Home, so far as any rent was concerned. They were simply luckless, inoffensive persons, whose improvidence would have run them ashore had they possessed the wealth of the Astors. They would willingly pay if they could. The family on the second floor had just lost a child, and the bread-winner of another little flock, the machinist, was sympathetically off his job in consequence of a strike on the part of the paper-makers. And so on to the end of the chapter.

How other owners of tenement property would act in such emergencies Mr. Shaw did not know; but he had a clear perception of his own helplessness. To proceed to extreme measures was repugnant to him. To let things go on as they were going meant the collapse of his scheme.

Mr. Shaw began to feel that he was not of the stuff out of which energetic and successful landlords are made. He was not, and the inmates of The Maria Home were aware of it. They belonged to a class which, however lacking in other gifts, does not lack the gift of character reading. Mrs. Malone, for illustration, had not required four weeks, or four minutes, to discover that she need not pay her rent regularly. She settled that point the instant she laid eyes on him. "It's a soft-natured man he is entirely," was her rapid diagnosis; "he looks like a born tyrant, he does, but he's no sand."

We shall not follow Mr. Shaw in his various troubles and embarrassments growing out of the financial problem. It was October, and the family was again in town. At the end of this month wholly new complications had arisen. Mrs. Malone and the Downeys were quarreling. The Downeys, having a harmonium, could not stand her assumptions of social superiority. One day happening on the ground at the crisis, Mr. Shaw overheard this fragment of dialogue:

"I've a cousin in the insurance," Mrs. Malone was saying haughtily, "a cousin once removed."

"Yes," retorted Delia, the younger Downey girl, "the police removed him!" — and Mr. Shaw with a heavy sigh hastened from the field of conflict. Whenever Mrs. Malone and any of the Downeys now met on the staircase there was sure to be a lively interchange of incivilities. This was annoying, and still more annoying was a case of musical intoxication that broke out on the third floor rear. The man kept everybody awake all night — singing national anthems and informing the neighborhood that Columbia was "the germ of the ocean."

"Here am I," reflected Mr. Shaw, "trying to ease a bit the burdens of these people, and there 's hardly one of them will lend a hand. It 's difficult to help the poor, but it is the poor that often make it difficult. They 're a blessed study. I don't see but they have just as good a time as anybody."

Bickerings upstairs and sporadic outbreaks of conviviality downstairs were greatly distressing Mr. Shaw, when a real disaster befell The Maria Home. Mr. Morrison, the silent and punctual Mr. Morrison, was arrested for complicity in a bank robbery over in Newark, and taken handcuffed from the house by a couple of detectives. A group of street arabs sent up a derisive cheer as the convoy descended the steps, and little Jimmy Dowd, the bootblack with one suspender, gave vent to his ecstatic delight by standing on his head on the curbstone. The Maria Home figured in the morning papers, and Mr. Shaw passed a sleepless night. A reporter had wanted to interview him! The unfortunate affair could not be kept from Mrs. Shaw and Elizabeth, as other disagreeable occurrences had been. It was too flagrant. While reading the police report, that morning, the young girl felt a heavy blight creeping over her Christmas tree.

"Fancy that quiet Mr. Morrison being a bank robber!" cried Elizabeth, not untouched by the lurid romance of it. "He must have broken into a great many banks, papa."

"I don't doubt it, my dear. That enabled him to pay his rent punctually, so perhaps we ought n't to complain. I almost wish Miss Delia Downey would blow up a safe or two," added Mr. Shaw, with bitter cheerfulness. "The firm of Maria and Company will go into insolvency if she does n't."

"Why, papa, I thought everything in that way was going just lovely."

"It looks it — at a distance. Looked at close to, everything is going to the dogs as fast as it can;" and Mr. Shaw vaguely passed one hand over what Elizabeth called his scalp-lock — a gesture always indicative of extreme discouragement.

It had become plain to Mr. Shaw that his only course was to put the Home into the hands of some agent who could run it properly. He himself had signally failed. In spite of all his precautions as to references, he had filled the house with a set of irresponsible and reckless persons, who, in addition to disgracing the place, paid little or nothing for the privilege. He was meditating the step when he was forced to immediate action by the illness of Mrs. Shaw, who had been ordered to spend the coming winter in a warm climate as the sole remedy. The Shaws had never been abroad, and the south of France was suggested.

Mr. Shaw looked about for some one competent to take charge of The Maria Home, and found him close at hand in the person of Mr. Swartz, the shrewd and not unkindly German grocer, who, belonging to the class with which he had to deal, would know how to manage them. In fact, the man had already been tacitly accepted by Mr. Shaw as a sort of agent. It was Mr. Swartz who secured occupants for the suite vacated by the Morrisons. Mr. Shaw instructed him to use the tenants with every consideration and kindness, but not to allow any one to remain who had fallen two months in arrears, unless it happened to be Mrs. Ward. Mr. Swartz promised to follow all instructions to the letter, and assured Mr. Shaw that he would have no non-paying tenants when he got back.

"Der rent is sheap, and dose peoples should pay on der top of der nail, vas n't it?" said Mr. Swartz, plunging recklessly into an alien idiom.

"Yes, Swartz, they should pay on the nail, as you say; but I'm afraid that they won't contrive to do it always. You must n't press them too hard. Give them a little time. Good-by, Swartz."

"Gott in himmel!" said Mr. Swartz, looking after Mr. Shaw as he went down the street; "vot a man! vot a lan'lordt!"

Mr. Shaw drew a deep breath of relief that bleak December morning as he stepped into the carriage that was to take him and Mrs. Shaw and Elizabeth to the steamer. Of their winter on the Continent this record makes no note.

The Shaws returned to New York early in the following spring. They reached West Fifteenth Street in the forenoon, and as soon as lunch was over Mr. Shaw set forth for The Maria Home, touching which he had had a sudden relapse of anxiety; for, from the moment Sandy Hook melted out of sight on the horizon until the moment when it came mistily into view again, he had troubled himself little about the tenement house. Though his agent's reports had at first been regular, if not always lucid — Swartz was the master of a phenomenal English prose style—Mr. Shaw had scarcely glanced at them. But now he remembered that it was more than two months since Mr. Swartz had given any signs of life, and the reflection brought a swift sense of uneasiness.

When Mr. Shaw found himself in front of The Maria Home he stood transfixed with amazement. The house was changed almost beyond recognition, and apparently unoccupied. There was not a window-blind remaining above the first story, the door of the grocery in the basement had been boarded up, and theatre posters decorated the dead spaces of the lower brickwork. What had happened? What had become of Swartz? What had become of everybody?

In such neighborhoods the corner drug-store is the vital centre of information. There was one on the next block, and thither Mr. Shaw hurried. A communicative clerk was engaged at the moment in coating a batch of aromatic pills by rolling them in fine powder scattered on a glass slab. Did he know anything about the vacant tenement house down the street? Well, yes, he knew all there was to know. About a week ago the police turned out the whole precious menagerie, neck and heels. The keys were at the precinct station. The building belonged to a man named Shaw — a philanthropic freak. The clerk himself had never seen him. He was supposed to be abroad somewhere. The place had been left in charge of a Dutchman called Swartz, who fired all the old tenants because they did n't pay down, and replaced them with a tough set. There were junketings and rows every night, and the patrolman on that beat had a sweet time of it. Swartz took to drink, and was as bad as any of them. The street was n't what might be called a Sunday-go-to-meeting street, but the neighbors could n't stand the racket, and lodged complaints. Then the circus was closed. Two days before the raid Swartz had disappeared, and the shebeen was running itself. Could n't say what had become of Swartz; he drank up his grocery store; did n't leave anything but a bushel of potatoes and a canary-bird. Did hear that he'd gone back to Germany. The police were waiting for the owner to put in an appearance. They had n't bothered themselves much over the matter; it had rather amused them; but then "Shaw's Folly" had always amused the neighborhood.

"Ah! They call the tenement 'Shaw's Folly,' do they?" and Mr. Shaw, paying no heed to the clerk's answer, muttered, "I should n't wonder if it was!"

In listening to the drug-clerk's off-hand discourse Mr. Shaw had run though a whole gamut of emotions. The "philanthropic freak" had brought a faint smile to his lips, but the characterization of The Maria Home as a "shebeen" made him wince. He was by turns pained, mortified, and indignant. Was it not a high-handed proceeding on the part of the authorities to evict his tenants and shut up the house? Then he had to admit that the circumstances justified the step. What else could the police have done? Thanking the clerk for his obliging information, Mr. Shaw walked thoughtfully down the street.

At the police station Mr. Shaw obtained the keys after some delay, and retraced his steps to The Maria Home. The interior of the house was in keeping with the dilapidated outside. The mystery of the missing window-blinds was explained by the absence of the balusters and the baluster-rails of all the staircases. They had probably been used for firewood during the winter. In some places even the mop-boards were stripped off. Everywhere were dust, rubbish, and confusion. The musty air of the silent rooms, whence the huddled life had so lately departed, seemed palpitant with ghosts. Mr. Shaw looked round him with a rueful smile.

"Swartz has kept his word. He told me I should n't have any non-paying tenants when I got back!"

Mr. Shaw did not pursue his investigations beyond the second floor. He had seen all he cared to see, and learned all he cared to know. Swartz had fled, with or without the two months' rental; it did n't matter. The happy refuge, builded for a few of the unhappy, had been destroyed by the hands of those it had meant to shelter. It is seldom that a man has his wrecked dream presented to him in so tangible a form.

"If ever I try to start another tenement house on a philanthropic basis," said Mr. Shaw to himself, "may I be — caught doing it and stopped, by Maria or somebody! 'Shaw's Folly' — well, yes, that describes it. Yet some man will do this thing some day, and make it pay. The idea was there all right, though I have n't seemed to know how to work it out. Perhaps there was too much charity in my plan — the kind of charity that gives birth to paupers."

Mr. Shaw locked the front door and slowly descended the stone steps, which were littered with handbills and dried scraps of orange peel. Reaching the sidewalk, he lingered an instant, glanced up at the looming red-brick façade, and then turned his back on The Maria Home.

It was a failure, but it was one of those failures in which lie the seeds of success. A dim and scarcely recognized presentiment of this was Mr. Shaw's sole consolation.

That same afternoon old Mr. Elijah Shaw dropped down from Vermont as if on purpose to say: "I told you so! I knew that Augustus would tumble into some sort of foolishness sooner or later. There's an abandoned farm up in New Hampshire waiting for Augustus. What's the use!"

AN UNTOLD STORY

THE night was heavy with the scents of flowers distilled in the dampness; a band was playing under a pavilion on the further side of the garden; among the foliage hung hundreds of colored lights. The moon had risen, and in open spaces the overleaning sprays and branches were stamped in black on the asphalt walks, which, diverging right and left, led to fountains and cafés and secluded nooks. Here, after the heat of the day, the beauty and fashion of Budapest assemble for an hour or two to lounge, and eat ices, and get a breath of cool air. In the gay season, nearly every nation on earth contributes a costume or a singularity to the picturesque throng.

Within a dozen paces of the little iron table where I was seated, the Danube swept by almost flush with the stone coping. At this point the current is very strong, running at a speed of not less than five or six miles an hour. The spring floods, fed by the snows and rains of the Blocksberg, must, at times, I thought, test the strength of the buttresses of the airy bridges whose far-stretched threads of light were now repeating themselves in the water.

A sultry summer night, with scarcely wind enough to stir a leaf on the topmost bough, and only now and then a hasty breath, like a sigh, from the river. The crowds of promenaders were gathered about the music-stand, and I was virtually alone as I sat listening to the Strauss waltz and repeopling the height of the opposite shore with the hordes of turbaned Turks who stormed and took the place in 1526. Etched against the sky was a crumbling citadel — no longer solicitous of the straggling gray town that had crept up to it for protection; a sentinel fallen asleep ages and ages ago. From time to time a small boat glided across the broad strip of moonlight lying on the water, and vanished.

Suddenly a figure, the slender figure of a girl, rushed past me, so closely that I felt the wind of the flying drapery. An instant afterward she had thrown herself into the Danube. A dark shape, which the velocity of the current pressed against the masonry, was carried twenty or thirty yards down the stream almost before I could spring to my feet. As I did so, a policeman, who seemed to rise out of the ground in the shadow of an acacia tree, leaned over the low curbing and clutched at the outspread skirt, which had not yet lost its buoyancy. A moment later two other guardians reached the spot, and the girl was lifted from the river, insensible, and lay glittering on the greensward.

She was not more than eighteen or nineteen, a very beautiful girl, with the full, delicate lines which distinguish the Slav women of even the peasant class. Her black hair hung in strands about the throat and face, the pallor of which was further intensified by the deep fringe of her eyelashes. On one half-bared shoulder, where it had probably grazed the brickwork, was a bruise. She wore a robe of some soft white material, plainly made, but in the fashion of the hour. A narrow scarlet ribbon, the bow of which had slipped under the ear, encircled her neck; a ring set with a single stone sparkled on the forefinger of the right hand. There were no other attempts at personal adornment. The simplicity of the girl's dress, with its certain negative evidences of refinement, left her grade in life indeterminate. She might have been a lady's maid — or a duchess. Beauty knows no distinction.

The color had gone from the lips. They were slightly parted, as though she were smiling in her trance — if it was a trance. Could it be death? That seemed hardly probable under the circumstances; though so complex and delicate is the mechanism of the heart that a lighter shock than she had sustained may stop it. She had floated face downward, and there was some delay in lifting the body from the water; but not three minutes had elapsed between the desperate act and the rescue.

By this time a number of persons had collected, and there were many gesticulations and much chattering in French, Italian, and Hungarian, the import of which I could not catch, beyond an inference that the girl had been identified by one of the bystanders — a nondescript elderly person, with glasses, who seemed in no especial manner afflicted by what had occurred, but was appreciative of his own accidental importance. Subsequently I received the impression that the man found himself mistaken, and had relapsed into nobody again.

The lookers-on increased momentarily, drawn to the spot by some inscrutable instinct of sight-seeing. One of the undreamed-of penalties of the suicide is to become spectacular.

At the approach of a newcomer, a physician, the crowd respectfully drew aside, making place for him. His examination was of necessity superficial and preliminary. When it was ended he rose from his knee, and without speaking spread a handkerchief over the face, until then uncovered. The thin tissue adhered to the damp features and straightway moulded itself into a startling mask. The doctor briefly interrogated the three guards, made a few memoranda on his tablets, and departed. A little distance off — their curiosity partly overcoming their fear — stood a group of children in an attitude of hesitation, ready for instant flight, like a flock of timid sparrows.

The physician's departure was the signal for renewed chattering and gesticulation, in which a helmeted sergent de ville now joined, taking rapid notes, and occasionally pausing to wave the book over his head — an energetic sergent de ville. Then an interval of poignant silence ensued. Everybody waited. Presently four men appeared with a litter, and the girl was laid upon it, looking like a marble statue carved on some mediæval tomb, and was so borne away.

The cortège had hardly disappeared down the main avenue when a gentleman, evidently a person of consequence, came hurriedly from an opposite direction, a footman in livery following closely at his heels. On learning which path the bearers had taken the pair hastened after them.

The crowd dispersed as quickly as it had gathered, and I went back to my seat under the trees. The river flowed on in the moonlight; strains of music from the orchestra, and sounds of happy voices, softened by distance, drifted through the shrubbery. The cafés were emptying, and richly decked women and men in evening dress sauntered idly past. Nothing was changed in the *mise-en-scène* of half an hour before; all the fairy-like stage-properties were the same. The effacement of the tragedy was so complete that the swift, dark interlude had scarcely left a sense of its incongruity. It was like a dream that one recalls confusedly on awaking. Did I imagine this thing, awhile ago, as I sat drowsing in my chair with the untasted ice beside me? One tangible detail remained — the trampled greensward, yonder, where the body had lain, and the parapet splashed with water.

The next morning I searched the papers, such at least as were printed in French, for some item touching the occurrence, but found none. How came it that the taste of life so soon turned bitter on those young lips? Was it some lover who scorned her, or one from whose love she fled? To the heart of what man, walking the thronged streets of the city or dwelling alone in some adjacent suburb, did this piteous death send an intended pang? There was a kind of relief in knowing nothing more than I had witnessed. Perhaps the vague drama that pieced itself loosely together in my imagination was better than the reality would have been. A gloss of grim fact might have spoiled the finer text. As it was, the pathos and the mystery of it all haunted me, and followed me across the sea.

In the months that succeeded, the incident gradually faded out of my mind, and probably would never have detached itself from the blur of half-forgotten things if chance had not again brought me to the Hungarian capital. As the Orient Express was nearing Budapest the recollection of the girl who threw herself into the river two years before came abruptly into my thought, and insisted on staying there. The reminiscence was natural enough, time and place considered, but the obstinacy of it irritated me a little.

After dinner, that evening, I joined the promenaders in the garden. The small iron table, with its green-painted chair under the linden, was in the same place, and had quite the air of having kept itself unoccupied for me all this while. The river once more turned itself into silver and lapis lazuli as I looked. The military band was playing the old interminable waltz, and the same waiter took my order for an ice — it might have been the untasted ice of two years ago, re-frozen. The thing that had happened seemed weirdly on the point of happening over again. Sitting there I half expected a slender girlish figure to rush past me. At intervals the remembered face glimmered among the shadows under the acacia trees, — the face like a white rose drenched with rain.

My halt at Budapest was of the briefest — a break in a long eastward journey, to be resumed the following afternoon.

As I was driving to the station, the next day, a block in the crowded street brought my conveyance to a stand. Facing me on my right, and some eight or ten yards distant, was a landau wedged in a mass of carriages. The gold braid of the coachman and footman first caught my eye; then I glanced at the occupants of the carriage, a lady and a gentleman — and on them my gaze rested spellbound. It was the girl I had helped to drag from the river! The gentleman at her side and the footman on the box were the two men who had hurried into the garden that night just after the removal of the body. Excepting for them I might have discredited my eyes. I could not be mistaken in all three.

It was she — pale, as I remember her, but

now with an aureole of distinction which she had not seemed to wear in her forlorner state. I had seen only her Slavonic beauty. She was simply robed, as then, but now more richly, with a flash of diamonds at the wrist as she lifted one hand in a sudden imperious gesture to the driver of a vehicle behind her. There was, I fancied, something characteristic and temperamental in that gesture.

I had only a moment for observation. The impeded stream of traffic flowed again and the landau swept by, leaving a deepened mystery on my hands.

Here was a more complex drama than I had sketched in my imagination two years previously. Then I had been content with the commonplace plot of some poor girl deserted by her lover. But now? The play was not so simple as that. It involved subtler motive and action, and a different setting. There were new elements in the tragedy, and sharper contrasts to be considered.

These two persons were evidently persons of rank. On the panels of the landau was an heraldic blazon — a clue, if it had been possible for me to follow it. Who were they? Father and daughter, or husband and wife, or mistress and lover? I was not to know. I had caught a glimpse of one lurid page in the book of those two lives; then the volume had been closed, and, so far as I was concerned, sealed forever.

That shut book! It stands darkling on a shelf by itself in my library, unread, and never to be opened. In certain frequent moods I find myself tantalized beyond reason by its conjectural romance. I have read many a famous novel which has not had for me one half the charm that lies in that untold story.

THE CASE OF THOMAS PHIPPS

I

When Thomas Phipps had reached what are called the years of discretion it was plainly apparent to the naked eye that discretion had not arrived with the years. This was a matter of no surprise to those familiar with his childhood, for an unworldly lack of common sense had distinguished him from the cradle. At the age of six he began attendance at the little red-brick schoolhouse on the Hampton turnpike, where he grew into a long, lank youth, tranquilly accepting the impositions of his classmates and the severities of a series of masters. The younger boys got his marbles away from him, and the elder boys assimilated the greater portion of his lunch at recess. If he exchanged jackknives, he generally found himself the final possessor of the one with a broken blade or some other abnormal defect. He was a distressing mixture of innocence, conscientiousness, and obstinacy. There were unexpected moments when it was impossible to do anything at all with him. His amiability never deserted him in these intervals; but somehow wrapped up in his guileless, half-infantile smile was the intimation of a will of iron. Whenever this particular look came into Thomas Phipps's face, the young brigands of the red schoolhouse called a halt to their persecutions. If he chanced, in the midst of that engaging smile, to remark, "I don't think you 'd better fool with that oriole's nest in the old elm down by the pond," the oriole's nest escaped pillage for the time being. Unlike the average country lad, he was very gentle with all gentle creatures, having a sort of esoteric kinship with birds, squirrels, and mud-turtles.

The setting forth of these traits of his childhood renders a later description unnecessary; for the boy was father to the man.

When Thomas Phipps's schooldays were over, his uncle, Daniel Whipple, who had adopted him in infancy, set him to work on the farm. The estate, which was called Westside, lay on the outskirts of Hampton, and had been in the family since 1760. Deacon Whipple was a widower, with two daughters somewhat younger than Thomas, whose lines were considered to have fallen in pleasant places. He would probably inherit Westside, or a portion of it, and certainly marry one of the girls—Mary, of course; Martha Jane squinted. The logical neighborhood had long ago arranged the programme.

Daniel Whipple was suspected of being very wealthy, and known to be eccentric. Though not precisely an ill-natured person, he was a man of strong antipathies, and not popular — especially not popular with his four cousins living in the town. The adoption of Thomas Phipps by the deacon had not been approved at the time by the Fishleys, and as years wore on, establishing closer relations between uncle and nephew, the disapproval was not modified. When young Phipps was put into training evidently intended to fit him for the ultimate proprietorship of Westside, the spectacle was too painful for the Fishleys. An indirect remonstrance lighted the ready pyre of Deacon Whipple's wrath, and the Fishleys, so to speak, perished in the flames. They were brothers.

Thomas Phipps took to farm-work with seeming relish, and developed cleverness on one or two unsuspected lines. He showed considerable knack at carpentering, and did a job of painting on the old stables so skillfully that the over-busy local painter was not missed. But Thomas Phipps's interest in agricultural pursuits was only seeming. He hated the business with great cheerfulness, and his cheerfulness deceived the uncle. Perhaps Daniel Whipple received the largest surprise of his life on the morning of the day when Thomas Phipps attained his majority. He walked into the barn where the deacon was inspecting a very recent heifer, and said quietly:

"Uncle Dan'el, I don't think I like farming."

"Don't like what?"

"Farming. I intend to give it up."

"Give it up!" cried the deacon, letting go his hold on the heifer's left hind leg with such suddenness as to cause the little stranger to topple over in the straw. "Are you crazy, Thomas? What are you driving at?"

"I never meant to be a farmer. I mean to be a painter."

The deacon had not risen from his half-kneeling posture. He now stood up.

"You want to be one of those long-haired artist-fellows that come mooning about here summer-times?"

"No," said Thomas Phipps, with a laugh — a laugh which in another man would have rung out, but in him was perfectly noiseless. "I propose to be a painter on a larger scale — a house-painter."

"You are not in earnest — you fool!"

"In dead earnest, Uncle Dan'el."

"Then you'd better put a cold bandage on your head, and go to bed."

The conversation which ensued that morning — good-natured and obstinate on the part of the nephew, thunderous and charged with lightning on the part of the uncle — needs no recording. The story is told in Deacon Whipple's concluding sentence:

"Thomas Phipps, if that's your last word, I don't ever want to see you inside my house again."

"If you should happen to want any outside painting" — began Thomas, but the old gentleman was swinging across the ten-acre lot on his way to the house.

Thus Thomas Phipps gave up an existence of assured ease and relative luxury in order to become merely a house-painter dependent on a precarious daily wage. It required a Thomas Phipps to do that, at the moment of reaching the years of discretion.

II

The young man had sufficient means to enable him to set up a small shop, and he set it up in the main street diagonally opposite a sign bearing the legend: "J. Timmins, Painter & Glazier." Before deciding on this step Thomas Phipps had approached Mr. Timmins with an offer of services and additional capital, but Mr. Timmins had declined both, and the result was a new studio over the way.

Thomas Phipps's rather singular move stirred endless gossip in Hampton, and touched some queer sense of humor lying dormant in the place. He had always been a favorite in the town, and there was a readiness to take sides with him against Deacon Whipple, if the two had quarreled. Whether they had or not, and if they had, on what grounds, remained unexplained. Thomas Phipps kept his own counsel and left the problem to solve itself. He arranged his paint-pots and brushes, and placidly waited for business. Presently odd small jobs began to come in — mostly from customers in debt to Mr. Timmins. The pickings were meagre and not profitable.

About this time, providentially, a feverish real-estate boom broke out in Hampton, and hideous little one-story cottages with slated mansard roofs sprang up everywhere, like mushrooms. The two painters in town were not too many for the emergency. Mr. Timmins had to sink his pride, and ask occasional collaboration at the hands of his rival, who in other ways came in handsomely for a share of the prosperity, though his fortunes fell below the level of his opportunity.

Thomas Phipps, as a house-painter, would have been a great success if it had not been for Thomas Phipps. He had certain positive ideas touching the proper colors for a special house or barn, and his loose, conscientious candor in attempting to impress these excellent ideas on his patrons lost him more than one desirable commission. When the Hon. James Boodle, who was erecting a very pretentious mansion with a chubby tower, directed Phipps to paint the outside in three colors, the first story brown, the second story yellow, and the third story gray, Mr. Phipps, with characteristic tact, asked the great statesman if he wanted his house "to look like a zebra." Mr. Timmins laid on the three colors, and said not a word. Phipps never understood how that job came to slip through his fingers.

"At the start Boodle was wild to have me do the work, would n't hear of anybody else putting a brush to it, and then the first thing I knew Timmins had his ladder swung against the north gable, and was painting away for dear life. Boodle does n't seem to know his own mind, what there is of it, for more than two minutes together."

Several months before he left his uncle's bed and board Thomas Phipps had fallen in love with Postmaster Spinney's daughter — a young lady whose worldly possessions included nothing more tangible than her implicit belief in the goodness and miscellaneous superiority of Thomas Phipps. The sudden change in his circumstances affected neither her faith nor her devotion.

> "Love is not love
> Which alters when it alteration finds"

in the once satisfactory annual stipend of the beloved. Miss Ethel Spinney held to her promise, though Postmaster Spinney would have liked to shirk his, given in the days of the suitor's prosperity. Mr. Thomas Phipps, the adopted son and presumably one of the heirs of Deacon Daniel Whipple, and Tom Phipps, the house-painter (when he could get any houses to paint), were two distinct individuals. The second had obliterated the first; but the first might suddenly come back and obliterate the second. The chances of this happening greatly unsettled Mr. Spinney, who at last gave a reluctant consent to Ethel's marriage. The modest wedding took place in the bride's home, and was unattended by any of the Westside people. Deacon Whipple never recognized Thomas Phipps on the street, and the girls only nodded to him furtively when they met. Of late they had ceased to do that. The alienation was complete.

Whether or not young Phipps's desertion interfered with any matrimonial plan of his uncle was guesswork. The offense need not have been so deep as that in order permanently to anger the deacon. In his dealings with mankind he was not tolerant of even slight opposition, though it was understood that the two Whipple girls could lead him with a hair. If this were so, they evidently did not exert their influence in making the deacon forgive his nephew. Was that through pique or indifference? Hampton was divided on the question.

The flush times had set Thomas Phipps on his feet in a way. He had bought and furnished a cottage, not much bigger than a bird-cage, in the part of the town to which fashion seemed to be wending her capricious steps. But before fashion reached his door, if she ever seriously intended to reach there, the building mania spent itself. Architectural zebras ceased to propagate in Hampton. Every kind of trade slackened, and Thomas Phipps would soon have acquired the hand of little employment had he not added carriage and sign painting to his preferred occupation.

As it was, domestic economy had to sail very close to the wind in Willow Street, the site of the bird-cage. Mrs. Phipps was an ingenious little housewife, and could make a palatable stew out of almost nothing; but she could not make a stew out of nothing at all, and that was the chief ingredient in prospect. She had the pluck that is hereditary in unspoiled New England country girls ; but now and then she broke down when alone, never in Thomas Phipps's presence. There was always a bright face when he came home from his work or no work. One evening, however, she sounded a desponding note in spite of herself.

"Tom," she said, "sometimes I think that you have n't been quite wise. You have n't looked out for yourself as sharply as other folks do who are n't really half so clever. If you had stayed up at Westside you 'd have been a rich man some day."

"Well," said Thomas Phipps, with an introspective air, "I was n't adapted to farming. I had n't any especial call on Uncle Dan'el's property, and I did n't want to marry Mary or Martha Jane. What I wanted, principally, was to marry Ethel Spinney."

"You did it, Tom."

"And I 'm not regretting it a minute," said Thomas Phipps. "Just pin that inside your sun-bonnet."

If Thomas Phipps had spells of depression, he was never caught in the act, at home or abroad. Frequently he could be observed standing in the doorway of his paint-shop and smiling like a multi-millionaire on the passers in the street. If Deacon Whipple chanced to drive by in his gig, Thomas would make him a friendly and respectful salutation, which was never returned. Then Thomas would indulge in one of his mute laughs.

"I 'm going to bow to Uncle Dan'el just as long as there 's anything left of both of us. I know I disappointed him, but I don't see why he takes it so hard. With his gray-colored sense of fun, I should think he 'd be amused. I had to do what I did, or I would n't ever have been happy."

Fortunately, the idea that he was not happy never once occurred to Thomas Phipps. It might have depressed him.

III

One morning, about eighteen months after his marriage, Thomas Phipps said to himself: "I begin to believe that true art is n't appreciated in Hampton. There 's a lack of inside and outside taste. Some things I can't and won't do. Timmins is the man for this locality. He 'd paint a cottage dead black if they told him to. A sky-blue hearse with pink dots would just suit him. Perhaps there 'd be a chance for me in a city like Portland or Portsmouth, if I could once find a footing."

The situation had become embarrassing.

He was too poor to remain in Hampton, and too poor to get away. This compromise was possible — Ethel might visit her mother for a week or ten days while he was prospecting elsewhere. Phipps involuntarily made a wry face as the thing suggested itself to him. "I 've never been separated from Ethel," he reflected, forgetting that he had been separated from her about nineteen years the day he married her.

Thomas Phipps had just taken down the shutters of the single window that lighted his shop, and was now sitting on an empty turpentine barrel near the open door facing the street. His mood was one of unwonted abstraction, for reverie was not in his line. Suddenly a chaise drew up at the curbstone, a man descended from the vehicle and mounted the three wooden steps leading from the sidewalk up to the narrow platform in front of the building. Phipps lifted his head and nodded pleasantly, wondering what brought Lawyer Dunn to the shop. As the gentleman was a bachelor, and boarded with the Odells, it was n't a job of painting.

"Mr. Phipps," said Mr. Dunn, speaking hurriedly, "Deacon Whipple has just been found dead in his carriage."

"Why — why, it was n't half an hour ago I saw him drive past!"

"What has happened must have happened as he reached the gate of his own house, or very shortly before. The horse was discovered standing quietly beside the hitching-post."

"Is n't there a mistake? Are you sure it is n't a faint, or something he 'll come out of?"

"Quite sure. It was a heart stroke. He is dead."

Thomas Phipps leaned against the door jamb and remained silent. Mr. Dunn turned to go, then lingered a moment, hesitating, and said: "Perhaps I ought to inform you that the will is to be examined this afternoon."

"This afternoon! Is not that rather quick?"

"It is rather unusual. Mr. Whipple had some unconventional notions, and this is one which we are constrained to respect. About a year ago he gave me written as well as oral commands to have the will opened immediately upon his demise — within three or four hours afterwards, if practicable, and in any event it was to be done previous to the interment. You will naturally desire to be present. I shall send word to the Fishleys."

"Well, I don't know," replied Thomas Phipps slowly. "I don't much care to go up to the house yet awhile. I guess I 'll wait for the funeral, unless I can be of any help. Perhaps they 'll send for me."

"Of course your attendance at the reading is not obligatory or any way necessary."

"I expect not. But I 'd half like to see the disappointment of the Fishleys."

"That is at your option."

As Mr. Dunn stepped into the chaise Thomas Phipps began to put up his shutters.

"I guess I 'll let the Fishleys enjoy it by themselves."

That afternoon the will was read to a silent group assembled in the half-darkened sitting-room at Westside, and an hour later every detail of the document was known to the town of Hampton. Nobody had suspected how rich he was — not even the tax assessors. There were several public bequests, which excited only passing comment. As a matter of course Deacon Whipple would remember the Baptist Church and the Infirmary. But the seventh clause of the will caused a sensation. In clause VII, a sum of $3000 was bequeathed to each of the Fishleys, and the sum of $1000 to Thomas Phipps. The astonishing feature was the condition attached to these legacies — *i. e.* that none of the five named legatees should attend the testator's funeral services, either at the house, the church, or the cemetery. In case this condition was not complied with by one or several of the above-named legatees, the executors of the will were empowered to carry out the sealed instructions left in the hands of the testator's lawyer, Silas Dunn.

In view of so remarkable a provision the correlative circumstance of Deacon Whipple's death was almost lost sight of. On the post-office steps, at the street corner, by the fire-side, and in Warner's drug-store — a centre of incandescent gossip — nothing was spoken of but the odd combination of generosity and malice embodied in that seventh clause.

"It 's the first time I ever heard of folks being hired to stay away from a funeral," observed Mr. Millet, the sexton of St. John's. He had an uneasy feeling that a slight had been cast upon him professionally.

"I wish somebody 'd hire me to stay away from mine," put in the local humorist.

"If you could, I don't know any man in town who would hire you," replied the branch-telegraph operator.

"Mebby some creditor," suggested a voice on the edge of the crowd.

Postmaster Spinney ventured to express the opinion that the parties interested in section VII would n't be likely to flock to the obsequies.

"I should smile," said the Hon. James Boodle.

"It's a windfall for Tom Phipps," remarked Selectman Devens; "not much of a one, considering; but a windfall's a windfall."

A broad smile overspread the township of Hampton when it was reported that Thomas Phipps had no intention whatever of conforming to his late uncle's wishes in the matter. The report was instantly credited. It was so like Tom Phipps to kick over his own pail of milk. It had been his chief occupation ever since he was five years old, and dazzling success had crowned his efforts. After blighting all his prospects by quitting Westside, no act of short-sightedness on his part was likely to take Hampton wholly by surprise. Of course he would go to that funeral, with his eyes wide open, and lose what little the old gentleman had designed to leave him. If the world had been populated exclusively by human beings like Tom Phipps, the whole concern would have been wound up long before the Deluge. Somebody ought to get hold of the idiot, and sit on his head for an hour or two while they were burying the Deacon.

"Such stupidity," declared Mr. Manners, the preceptor of the Boys' High School, "could not have been acquired; it must have existed in Mr. Phipps anterior to his birth."

"It seems to me," said Parson Hackett,

"that at times he has the air of acting quite independently of his own volition, impelled, as it were, by some outside occult influence. It 's not a question of free will with him. I think myself it was foreordained that he should attend the Deacon's funeral. He can't help doing it."

"Tom Phipps is a forgivin' angel, that 's what he is," said Miss Clarissa Simms, the milliner.

"Tom 's a good boy," assented young Melcher, who was paying attentions to Miss Clarissa; "but as for a downright angel, I don't think he 's got more 'n his pin-feathers jest yet."

Phipps had said nothing to Ethel on the subject, and she had not ventured to question him. The rumor came to her from outside; but she believed it, and knew herself to be powerless. If he had made up his mind, it was no use talking. Ethel watched him nervously that afternoon and all the next day. Either because he scorned so small a legacy, or because he could n't resist the temptation to do an unwise thing, Tom was going to that funeral. And they were so poor!

Deacon Whipple had died on a Monday, and the services were appointed for Wednesday. On that morning Thomas Phipps dressed himself in his Sunday suit and carefully knotted a black silk necktie, an article which had not hitherto figured as an item in his limited wardrobe. By what piece of Jay-Gouldish financiering this necktie and a pair of sombre gloves were accumulated remains a secret. On the day of his marriage he had not arrayed himself with more pains.

Ethel sat on the side of the bed, mutely watching every movement. When his toilet was completed and he turned towards the door, she slowly rose to her feet.

"Tom, do you really mean to — to — "

"I must, Ethel. If I 'm built lop-sided I must go as I 'm built — crooked. I 've thought the whole miserable business over till my head aches, and I don't see any two ways of acting. Uncle Dan'el had his faults; at times he was a hard man; but he was good to me when I was a boy, and not ten thousand dollars, let alone ten hundred, could keep me from going to his funeral. Uncle Dan'el did n't mean I should have a cent. He knew me down to the ground, and he knew I was n't going to swallow any such bitter pill as he 'd put up for me. Self-respect comes high, but I 've got to have it. It 's about the only thing that 's worth what it costs — that and first-class linseed oil."

"You're not like other people, Tom, and perhaps that's why I love you. You seem to do the foolishest things, but somehow there's always a kind of right at the bottom of the foolishness, even when it does n't turn out well. At first I thought differently from you about this matter, but now I have n't a word to say. I don't care for that money if you don't. I just want you to be yourself." And as Ethel stood on tiptoe to straighten the black necktie there was only a suspicion of moisture in her eyes, and nothing of reproach.

She did not accompany Phipps to Westside, and was impatiently waiting for him at the street door when he returned home shortly after noontime.

"Were the Fishleys there?" was Ethel's first question.

"They were n't there in great numbers," replied her husband, smiling; "but all the rest of the population was on hand. I never saw such a crowd; it stretched out to the front gate. I'm glad I went."

"Did anybody say anything to you, Tom?"

"Parson Hackett shook hands with me, and Mr. Devens said he expected I'd turn up. Everybody turned up, even Li Fang. You know the old man helped him to start his laundry. It was funny to see the heathen Chinee standing round outside, dressed to kill, like an idol in a waxwork show. Li Fang looked kind of sad. They said he wanted to let off some fire-crackers as the coffin was brought out. He was blowing on a piece of lighted punk when they stopped him."

"Poor Li Fang! Perhaps he was the only sincere mourner in the whole lot, not counting Mary and Martha Jane, of course."

Nothing short of the fullest particulars would satisfy Ethel, and these Thomas Phipps gave her, suppressing the fact that his presence at the ceremonies had overshadowed the principal actor on the scene. The general interest had riveted itself on the droll spectacle of Thomas Phipps forfeiting his legacy. The young man's incomprehensible conduct was viewed in only one light. As he entered the room and quietly seated himself, his father-in-law leaned over and whispered to a neighbor:

"'Though thou shouldest bray a fool in a mortar among wheat with a pestle, yet will not his foolishness depart from him.'"

"Sure," was the low-toned rejoinder. "A gold mine would be throwed away on a crank like that."

That evening, after supper, Thomas Phipps broached his plan of going to Portland, or some other wider field, in search of an opening. He would of course be obliged to make the venture alone, Ethel to join him immediately in case of his success. Meanwhile Mrs. Spinney would not object to having her daughter back again for a week. Ethel at once assented to the arrangement. The project admitted of no delay.

"I'll put on my things now, and run over and tell mother," said Ethel.

"I'll go along with you. If they should n't happen to be pleased with the idea — "

"Oh, but they 'll be pleased!"

"I'll go along, anyway. I'd like to try to make your father understand how I feel about Uncle Dan'el. I doubt if I can."

He failed in that — neither of the Spinneys could understand it; but the proposition to have Ethel stay with them during Phipps's absence met their views. Though the young man wore a propitiatory smile, there was something about the thin compressed lips that prevented the Spinneys from fully expressing their minds on the burning subject of the will. They consoled themselves with the thought that no such diplomacy would be needed in the case of poor Ethel later on. They would leave her in no doubt as to their opinion of the imbecile she had got upon her hands. It would be a blessing if he were to take himself off for good. There was no longer any chance of his ever being anything but just Tom Phipps, the painter. Even if he had stayed from the funeral, it would n't have greatly mended the matter. What did ten hundred dollars amount to, when it might have been as many thousands?

Getting his daughter alone for a moment, Mr. Spinney said to her:

"I guess you 've got about enough of Tom Phipps for the present. A little of him goes a good ways, I should say. Don't wonder you want a change."

"Tom is very kind to me," replied Ethel demurely, with a flitting spark in either eye. "Of course a husband is n't like a tender, considerate father always on the lookout to save his daughter's feelings from every sort of hurt."

Mr. Spinney drew a quick breath, and gave Ethel a flurried glance. The velvet paw had suddenly scratched him.

IV

The next day Phipps began preparing for his departure. Late in the afternoon, as he was setting the shop to rights, Mr. Dunn drove up to the door and alighted.

"I hope nobody else is dead," was Thomas Phipps's swift reflection. He dusted off the seat of the only chair on the premises, and offered it to Mr. Dunn, who did not speak for full half a minute. Then he said:

"Mr. Phipps, in disregarding your late uncle's injunction you debarred yourself from receiving the legacy left to you conditionally in the seventh clause of his will."

"I understood that to be about the size of it. I 've been told so forty or fifty times since yesterday."

"Naturally. Your surprising procedure, if you will allow me so to characterize it, has resulted in rendering null and void that whole clause in the testament."

"No! I don't see how any act of mine could upset the bequests to the Fishleys. *They* did n't go to the funeral. Every one of 'em stuck to orders like a little man."

"They complied with the stipulations of the testament," said the lawyer, with a touch of asperity in his voice.

"That 's what I 'm saying. They sat right up and took their medicine."

"That 's the point. It was through no fault of theirs that they got debarred."

"It was my fault, then? I suppose it 's wicked in me, Mr. Dunn, but I 'm glad if the Fishleys are n't going to get anything, whatever way the matter came about. They don't deserve the money, and don't especially need it."

"Fortunately, they do not need it."

"They 'll put up a stiff fight all the same."

"I should not like to hold a brief for them. But this is a side issue of no interest."

"It 's all as interesting as can be."

"You were not at the reading of the will last Monday afternoon, and are perhaps unaware that in the seventh clause mention was made of supplementary instructions, consigned to my charge, for the executors to act upon in the not probable contingency of one or more of the beneficiaries named failing to respect the testator's wishes on a certain point."

"Yes, I heard about that."

"Well, Mr. Phipps, the astonishing step you took made the immediate examination of that paper imperative. It cancels the whole of section VII, and directs the executors to pay over the various sums therein specified to such person or persons (of the five legatees named) as should be present at the testator's funeral in spite of his prohibition — the aggregate sum to be divided share and share alike in case there should be two or more such persons. It is hardly necessary for me to say, Mr. Phipps, that the sum of thirteen thousand dollars falls to you."

The young man leaned back on the turpentine barrel, upon the head of which he had seated himself, and broke into one of those peculiar laughs of his — a laugh that could be seen but not heard.

"I always thought there was a heap of concealed fun in Uncle Dan'el," said Thomas Phipps. Then, with great seriousness: "I wish you'd break the news as gently as you can to father-in-law Spinney."

THE WHITE FEATHER

THE MAJOR'S STORY

In "The Thousand and One Nights" the vizier's daughter, Shahrazád, told all the stories; but in our single séance the tales were told by five men, gathered round the hearthstone of a New England roadside tavern, in which they had sought shelter from a blizzard and were snow-bound for the night. The sleighing party thus circumstanced found themselves, after supper, in a comfortable sitting-room with a blazing fire of hemlock logs in front of them, and for lack of more original entertainment fell to story-telling. Though each of the five narratives which then took shape in the firelight had its own proper *raison d'être*, I shall reproduce only one of them here. The narrative so specialized owes its consequence, such as it is, to the fact that the narrator — nearly a personal stranger to me — was obliged to leave it in a manner unfinished, and that I, by singular chance, was able to supply what might be called the sequel.

This story, which I have named "The White

Feather," was related by a Massachusetts veteran of the Civil War, who had left one arm behind him on the field and in the record of his regiment a reputation for great bravery. The Major, as I subsequently learned, had received a military education at a period when the army held out but scant inducements, and had turned aside from it to study law. At the beginning of hostilities in '61, he offered his services to the Federal government, and was placed upon the staff of General ——, with the rank of captain. The grade of major was afterward won in a Massachusetts regiment. Severely wounded at Spottsylvania Court House, and permanently disabled, he resigned his commission, and, after a long invalidism, took to the law again.

With the fullest claim to the later title of Judge, he prefers to be thought of and addressed as the Major. To-day, his sinewy, erect figure and clear blue eyes, gentle and resolute by turns behind their abattis of gray eyebrow, give no hint of his threescore years and ten, especially when he is speaking.

"Some men," began the Major, setting his half-emptied tumbler a little farther back from the edge of the table, "some men have a way of impressing us at sight as persons of indomitable will, or dauntless courage, or sterling integrity — in short, as embodiments of this or that latent quality, although they may have given no evidence whatever of possessing the particular attribute in question. We unhesitatingly assume how they would act under certain imaginable circumstances and conditions. A gesture, a glance of the eye, a something in the intonation of the voice, hypnotizes us, and we at once accept as real what may be only a figment of our own creating. My story, if it 's what you would call a story, deals incidentally with one of these curious prepossessions."

The Major paused a moment, and beat a soft tattoo with two fingers on the arm of the chair, as if he were waiting for his thoughts to fall into line.

"At the outbreak of the war, Jefferson Kane was in his senior year at West Point. The smoke of that first gun fired in Charleston harbor had hardly blown away when he withdrew from the Academy — to cast his lot, it was surmised, with that of his native state, as many another Southron in like circumstances was doing; for Kane belonged to an old Southland family. On the contrary, he applied for service in the army of the North — in the then nebulous Army of the Potomac. Men of his training were sorely needed at the moment, and his application was immediately granted.

"Kane was commissioned first lieutenant and provisionally assigned for duty in a camp of instruction somewhere in Massachusetts, at Readville, if I recollect. There he remained until the early part of '62, doing important work, for the recruits that passed through his hands came out finished soldiers, so far as drill was involved. Then Kane was ordered to the front, and there I fell in with him, — a tall, slender young man, with gray eyes and black hair, which he wore rather long, unlike the rest of us, who went closely cropped, Zouave fashion. I ought to say here that though I saw a great deal of him at this time, I am now aware that the impression he produced upon me was somewhat vague. His taking sides with the North presumably gave mortal offense to his family; but he never talked of himself or of the life he had left behind him in the South. Without seeming to do so, he always avoided the topic.

"From the day Kane joined our regiment, which formed part of Stahl's brigade, he was looked upon as a young fellow destined to distinguish himself above the common. It was no ordinary regiment into which he had drifted. Several of the companies comprising it were made up of the flower of New England youth —college seniors, professional men, men of wealth and social rating. But Kane was singled out from the throng, and stood a shining figure.

"I cannot quite define what it was that inspired this instant acceptance of him. Perhaps it was a blending of several things, — his judicial coolness, his soldierly carriage, the quiet skill and tact with which he handled men drawn from peaceful pursuits and new to the constraints of discipline; men who a brief space before were persons of consideration in their respective towns and villages, but were now become mere pawns on the great chess-board of war. At times they had to be handled gingerly, for even a pawn will turn. Kane's ready efficiency, and the modesty of it — the modesty that always hitches on to the higher gifts — naturally stimulated confidence in him. His magnetic Southern ways drew friends from right and left. Then he had the prestige of the West Pointer. But allowing for all this, it is not wholly clear what it was that made him, within the space of a month, the favorite of the entire regiment and the idol of Company A, his own company. That was the position he attained with apparently no effort on his part. Company A would have died for him, to a man. Among themselves, round the mess table, they did n't hide their opinion of Jeff Kane, or their views on the situation at large. The chief command would have been his, could the question have been put to vote. 'I would n't like to lose the kid out of the company,' observed Sergeant Berwick one day, 'but it would be a blessed good thing if he could change shoulder straps with the colonel.'"

Here the Major suddenly remembered the unfinished Bourbon and Apollinaris in his glass and interrupted himself.

"The colonel alluded to by the sergeant was a colonel of politics, and ought to have stuck to his glue factory down East. In those days we had a good many generals and colonels, and things, with political pulls. I think there were more than a few of that kidney in our recent little scrimmage with Spain. I don't believe in putting protégés and hangers-on out of employment over the heads of men who have been trained to the profession of arms. Some fine day we'll be convinced of the expediency of stowing the politicians. We ought to have a National Cold Storage Warehouse on purpose. But that's another story, as our friend Kipling remarks — too frequently."

The Major flicked off a flake of cigar ash from the looped-up empty sleeve that constantly gave him the oratorical air of having one hand thrust into his shirt-bosom, and went on with his narrative.

"We were as yet on only the outer edge of that lurid battle-summer which no man who lived through it, and still lives, can ever forget. Meanwhile vast preparations were making for another attempt upon Richmond. The inertia of camp-life with no enemy within reach tells on the nerves after a while. It appeared to be telling on young Kane's. Like the regiment, which hitherto had done nothing but garrison duty in forts around Washington, he had seen no active service, and was ready for it. He was champing on the bits, as the boys said. His impatience impressed his comrades, in whose estimation he had long since become a hero — with all the heroism purely potential.

"For months the monotony of our existence had been enlivened only by occasional reconnaissances, with no result beyond a stray minié ball now and then from some outlying sharpshooter. So there was widespread enthusiasm, one night, when the report came in that a large Confederate force, supposed to be Fitzhugh Lee, was in movement somewhere on our left. In the second report, which immediately telescoped the first, this large force dwindled down to a small squad thrown forward — from an Alabama regiment, as we found out later — to establish an advanced picket line. A portion of Company A was selected to look into the move, and dislodge or capture the post. I got leave to accompany Lieutenant Kane and the thirty-five men detailed for duty.

"We started from camp at about four o'clock of an ugly April morning, with just enough light in the sky to make a ghastly outline of everything, and a wind from the foothills that pricked like needles. Insignificant and scarcely noticed details, when they chance to precede some startling event, have an odd fashion of storing themselves away in one's memory. It all seems like something that happened yesterday, that tramp through a landscape that would have done credit to a nightmare — the smell of the earth thick with strange flowering shrubs; the overleaning branches that dashed handfuls of wet into our faces; the squirrel that barked at us from a persimmon tree, and how private Duffy raised a laugh by singing out, 'Shut up, ye young rebil!' and brought down upon himself a curt reprimand from Kane; for we were then beyond our own lines, and silence was wholesome. The gayety gradually died out of us as we advanced into the *terra incognita* of the enemy, and we became a file of phantoms stealing through the gloaming.

"Owing to a stretch of swamp and a small stream that tried to head us off in a valley, it was close upon sunrise when we reached the point aimed at. The dawn was already getting in its purple work behind the mountain ranges; very soon the daylight would betray us — and we had planned to take the picket by surprise. For five or ten minutes the plan seemed a dead failure; but presently we saw that we had them. Our approach had evidently not been discovered. The advantages were still in our favor, in spite of the daybreak having overtaken us.

"A coil of wet-wood smoke rising above the treetops, where it was blown into threads by the wind, showed us our nearness to the enemy. Their exact position was ascertained by one of our scouts, who crawled through the underbrush and got within a hundred feet of the unsuspecting bivouac.

"On the flattened crest of a little knoll, shut in by dwarf cedars and with a sharp declivity on the side opposite us, an infantry officer and twelve or fifteen men were preparing to breakfast. In front of a hut built of boughs and at some distance from the spot where the rifles were stacked, a group in half undress was sniffing the morning air. A sentinel, with his gun leaning against a stump, was drinking something out of a gourd as unconcernedly as thank you. Such lack of discipline and utter disregard of possible danger were common enough in both armies in the early days of the war. 'The idea of burning green wood on a war-path!' growled the scout. 'If them tenderfoots was in the Indian country their scalps would n't be on their empty heads a quarter of an hour.'

"We did n't waste a moment preparing to rush the little post. A whispered order was passed along not to fire before we sprang from cover, and then the word would be given. There was a deathly stillness, except that the birds began to set up a clatter, as they always do at dawn. I remember one shrill little cuss that seemed for all the world to be trying to sound a note of alarm. We scarcely dared draw breath as we moved stealthily forward and up the incline. The attacking party, on the right, was led by Kane, and comprised about two thirds of the detachment; the remainder was to be held in reserve under me. The row of cedars hung with creeper hid us until we were within forty or fifty yards of the encampment, and then the assaulting column charged.

"What happened then — I mean the dark and fatal thing that happened — I did n't witness; but twenty pairs of eyes witnessed it, and a score of tongues afterward bore testimony. I did not see Lieutenant Kane until the affair was over.

"Though the Confederates were taken wholly unawares, the first shot was fired by them, for just as our men came into the open the sentinel chanced to pick up his musket. A scattering volley followed from our side, and a dozen gray figures, seen for a moment scuttling here and there, seemed to melt into the smoke which had instantly blotted out nearly everything. When the air cleared a little, Kane's men were standing around in disorder on the deserted plateau. A stack of arms lay sprawling on the ground and an iron kettle of soup or coffee, suspended from a wooden tripod, was simmering over the blaze of newly lighted fagots. How in the devil, I wondered, had the picket-guard managed to slip through their hands? What had gone wrong?

"It was only on the return march that I was told, in broken words, what had taken place. Lieutenant Kane had botched the business — he had shown the white feather! The incredible story took only a few words in the telling.

"Kane had led the charge with seeming dash and valor, far in advance of the boys, but when the Confederate officer, who was pluckily covering the flight of the picket, suddenly wheeled and with sweeping sabre rushed toward Kane, the West Pointer broke his stride, faltered, and squarely fell back upon the line hurrying up the slope to his support. The action was so unexpected and amazing that the men came to a dead halt, as if they had been paralyzed in their tracks, and two priceless minutes were lost. When the ranks recovered from their stupor, not a gray blouse was anywhere to be seen, save that of the sentry lying dead at the foot of the oak stump.

"That was the substance of the hurried account given me by Sergeant Berwick. It explained a thing which had puzzled me not a little. When I reached the plateau myself, immediately after the occurrence of the incident, Kane's men were standing there indecisive, each staring into his comrade's face in a dazed manner. Then their eyes had turned with one accord upon Lieutenant Kane. That combined glance was as swift, precise, and relentless as a volley from a platoon. Kane stood confronting them, erect, a trifle flushed, but perfectly cool, with the point of his sabre resting on the toe of one boot. He could n't have appeared cooler on a dress-parade. Something odd and dramatic in the whole situation set me wondering. The actors in the scene preserved their hesitating attitude for only twenty seconds or so, and then the living picture vanished in a flash, like a picture thrown from the kinetoscope, and was replaced by another. Kane stepped forward two paces, and as his sword cut a swift half-circle in the air, the command rang out in the old resonant, bell-like tones, 'Fall in, men!' I shall never forget how he looked every inch the soldier at that moment. But they — they knew!

"There was no thought of pursuing the escaped picket with the chances of bringing up against an entire regiment, probably somewhere in the neighborhood. The men silently formed into line, a guard was detailed to protect the rear of the column, and we began our homeward march.

"That march back to Camp Blenker was a solemn business. Excepting for the fact that we were on the double-quick and the drum taps were lacking, it might have been a burial. Not a loud word was spoken in the ranks, but there was a deal of vigorous thinking. I noticed that Second Lieutenant Rollins and three or four others never took their eyes off of Jefferson Kane. If he had made a motion to get away, I rather fancy it would have gone hard with him.

"We got into camp on schedule time, and in less than fifteen minutes afterward Jefferson Kane's name was burning on every lip. Marconi's wireless telegraph was anticipated that forenoon in Camp Blenker. On a hundred intersecting currents of air the story of the lieutenant's disgrace sped from tent to tent throughout the brigade.

"At first nobody would believe it — it was some sell the boys had put up. Then the truth began to gain ground; incredulous faces grew serious; it was a grim matter. The shadow of it gathered and hung over the whole encampment. A heavy gloom settled down upon the members of Company A, for the stigma was especially theirs. There were a few who would not admit that their lieutenant had been guilty of cowardice, and loyally held out to the end. While conceding the surface facts in the case, they contended that the lieutenant had had a sudden faint, or an attack of momentary delirium. Similar instances were recalled. They had happened time and again. Anybody who doubted the boy's pluck was an idiot. A braver fellow than Jeff Kane never buckled a sword-belt. That vertigo idea, however, did n't cut much ice, as you youngsters of to-day would phrase it. There were men who did not hesitate to accuse Lieutenant Kane of intending to betray the detachment into the hands of the Confederates. Possibly he did n't start out with that purpose, it might have occurred to him on the spot; the opportunity had suggested it; if there had been more than a picket-guard on hand he would have succeeded. But the dominant opinion was summed up by Corporal Simms: 'He just showed the white feather, and that's all there is about it. He did n't mean nothin', he was just scared silly.'

"In the mean time Kane had shut himself in his tent on the slant of a hill, and was not seen again, excepting for half a moment when he flung back the flap and looked down upon the parade ground with its radiating white-walled streets. What report he had made of the expedition, if he had made any report, did not transpire. Within an hour after our return to camp a significant meeting of the captains of the regiment had been convened at headquarters. Of course a court-martial was inevitable. Though Lieutenant Kane had not as yet been placed under actual arrest, he was known to be under surveillance. At noon that day, just as the bugle was sounding, Jefferson Kane shot himself."

The Major made an abrupt gesture with his one hand, as if to brush away the shadow of the tragedy.

"That was over forty years ago," he continued meditatively, "but the problem discussed then has been discussed at odd intervals ever since. In a sort of spectral way, the dispute has outlasted nine tenths of those who survived the war. Differences of opinion hang on like old pensioners or the rheumatism. Whenever four or five graybeards of our regiment get together, boring one another with 'Don't you remember,' the subject is pretty sure to crop up. Some regard Kane's suicide as a confession of guilt, others as corroborative proof of the mental derangement which first showed itself in his otherwise inexplicable defailance before a mere handful of the enemy — a West Pointer ! So we have it, hot and heavy, over a man who nearly half a century ago ceased to be of any importance."

"What is your own diagnosis of the case, Major ?" asked young Dr. Atwood, who always carried the shop about with him.

"Personally," returned the Major, "I acquit Kane of disloyalty, and I don't believe that he was exactly a coward. He had n't the temperament. I will confess that I'm a little mixed. Sometimes I imagine that that first glimpse of his own people somehow rattled him for an instant, and the thing was done. But whether that man was a coward or a traitor, or neither, is a question which has never definitely been settled."

"Major," I said, hesitating a little, "I think I can, in a way, settle it — or, at least, throw some light upon it."

"You ?" —and the Major, with a half-amused

air, looked up at me from under his shaggy, overhanging eyebrows. "Why, you were not born when all this happened."

"No, I was not born then. My knowledge in the matter is something very recent. While wintering in the South, two or three years ago, I became acquainted, rather intimately acquainted, with the family of Jefferson Kane — that is, with his brother and sister."

"So?"

"It was not until after the surrender of Lee that Jefferson's death was known as a certainty to his family — the manner of it is probably not known to them to this hour. Indeed, I am positive of it. They have always supposed that he died on the field or in the hospital."

"The records at the War Department could have enlightened them," said the Major.

"They did not care to inquire. He had passed out of their lives, his defection never was forgiven. The Confederate officer before whose sword Lieutenant Kane recoiled that day was his father."

"So!"

"Captain Peyton Kane was a broken man after that meeting. He never spoke of it to a living soul save one — his wife, and to her but once. Captain Kane was killed in the second day's battle at Gettysburg."

My words were followed by a long silence. The room was so still that we could hear the soft pelting of the snow against the window-panes.

Then the old Major slowly rose from the chair and took up the empty glass beside him, not noticing that it was empty until he had lifted it part way to his lips. "Boys," he said, very gently, "only blank cartridges are fired over soldiers' graves. Here 's to their memory — the father and the son!"

Other stories, mirthful and serious, were told later on; but the Major did not speak again. He sat there in the dying glow of the firelight, inattentive, seemingly remote in an atmosphere of his own, brooding, doubtless, on

> "Old, unhappy, far-off things,
> And battles long ago."

INDEX TO TITLES OF THE PROSE WORKS

Affectation, On a Certain, ix. 91.
Asides, ix. 43.
Autograph Hunter, The, ix. 108.

Case of Thomas Phipps, The, ix. 273.
Chevalier de Resseguier, The, iii. 244.
Christmas Fantasy, with a Moral, A, vii. 304.
Cornwall, Barry, Leigh Hunt and, ix. 69.
Cruelty of Science, The, ix. 64.

Decoration Day, ix. 74.

Early Rising, On, ix. 79.

Fleabody and Other Queer Names, ix. 54.
For Bravery on the Field of Battle, v. 263.
From Ponkapog to Pesth, viii. 1.

Goliath, iii. 226.

Her Dying Words, iii. 272.
Herrick, Robert, ix. 115.
His Grace the Duke, ix. 194.
Historical Novels, ix. 100.
Hunt, Leigh, and Barry Cornwall, ix. 69.

L'Aiglon, A Note on, ix. 57.
Leaves from a Note Book, ix. 1.
Little Violinist, The, vii. 281.

Mademoiselle Olympe Zabriski, iii. 116.
Male Costume of the Period, The, ix. 87.
Marjorie Daw, iii. 1.
Midnight Fantasy, A, iii. 82.
Miss Mehetabel's Son, iii. 45.
My Cousin the Colonel, v. 203.

Note Book, Leaves from a, ix. 1.
Note on L'Aiglon, A, ix. 57.

Old Town by the Sea, An, viii. 175.
On a Certain Affectation, ix. 91.
On Early Rising, ix. 79.
Our New Neighbors at Ponkapog, vii. 295.

Père Antoine's Date-Palm, iii. 294.
Plot and Character, ix. 62.
Poête Manqué, Un, ix. 83.
Ponkapog Papers, ix. 1.
Ponkapog to Pesth, From, viii. 1.
Poor Yorick, ix. 103.
Prudence Palfrey, iv. 1.

Queen of Sheba, The, v. 1.
Quite So, iii. 158.

Rivermouth Romance, A, iv. 269.

Sea Turn, A, ix. 151.
Shaw's Folly, ix. 211.
Stillwater Tragedy, The, vi. 1.
Story of a Bad Boy, The, vii. 1.
Struggle for Life, A, iii. 139.

Tom Folio, ix. 45.
Two Bites at a Cherry, iii. 181.

Untold Story, An, ix. 263.

White Feather, The, ix. 298.
Wishmakers' Town, ix. 95.
Writers and Talkers, ix. 77.

Yorick, Poor, ix. 103.

The Riverside Press
CAMBRIDGE . MASSACHUSETTS
U · S · A